THE AMERICAN ASSEMBLY
Columbia University
in cooperation with
THE BROOKINGS INSTITUTION
and THE URBAN INSTITUTE

Updating America's Social Contract

Economic Growth and Opportunity in the New Century

Rudolph G. Penner
Isabel V. Sawhill
Timothy Taylor

W. W. Norton & Company
New York • London

The text of this book is composed in Baskerville
Composition by Allentown Digital Services Division of
R.R. Donnelley & Sons Company
Manufacturing by The Haddon Craftsmen, Inc.

Library of Congress Cataloging-in-Publication Data

Penner, Rudolph Gerhard, 1936–
Updating America's social contract : economic growth and opportunity in
the new century / Rudolph G. Penner, Isabel V. Sawhill, Timothy Taylor.
p. cm.—(Uniting America—toward common purpose)
"This volume was prepared as a background for an Assembly of
forty-eight leaders . . . that met at the Emory University
Conference Center in Atlanta, June 10–13, 1999."
At head of title: The American Assembly.
Includes index.
ISBN 0-393-97579-7 (pbk.)
1. Income distribution—United States. 2. Industrial productivity—United States.
3. United States—Economic conditions—1993– 4. Economic forecasting—
United States. 5. United States—Social conditions—1980– I. Sawhill, Isabel V.
II. Taylor, Timothy. III. American Assembly. IV. Title. V. Series.

HC110.I5 P39 2000
306'.0973—dc21   00-028364

W. W. Norton & Company, Inc., 500 Fifth Avenue, New York, N.Y. 10110
www.wwnorton.com

W. W. Norton & Company Ltd., 10 Coptic Street, London WC1A 1PU

1 2 3 4 5 6 7 8 9 0

Updating America's

Social Contract

THE AMERICAN ASSEMBLY was established by Dwight D. Eisenhower at Columbia University in 1950. Each year it holds at least two nonpartisan meetings that give rise to authoritative books that illuminate issues of United States policy.

An affiliate of Columbia, the Assembly is a national, educational institution incorporated in the state of New York.

The Assembly seeks to provide information, stimulate discussion, and evoke independent conclusions on matters of vital public interest.

Contents

Preface

The American Assembly commissioned this volume to contribute to the national debate about the key long-term issues facing the U.S. economy in the opening decades of the twenty-first century. The U.S. economy performed strongly in the 1990s, producing one of the longest economic expansions of the century, reducing unemployment and inflation rates to levels not seen for decades, driving the stock market to new highs, and perhaps most surprising of all, creating enough additional tax revenue to turn the federal budget deficits of the last several decades into surpluses. Some have gone so far as to argue that a "new economy" has arrived, driven by forces like new technology and globalization, which will generate this sort of economic good news for years to come.

However, even in the midst of this almost continual stream of economic good news, several nagging long-term issues remain:

• First, the average annual rate of productivity growth, which is the key determinant of increases in the standard of living over time, has been relatively low since the early 1970s. Although productivity growth did seem to perk up in the late 1990s, it is uncertain whether this represents a short-term blip or a fundamental change.

• Second, concerns have arisen over the degree of inequality and opportunity amidst America's growing prosperity. The distribution of household income became more uneven between the 1970s and the early 1990s; although inequality is no longer growing in the late 1990s, it is still higher than it was in the 1970s. Further, as a result of the weakening of family ties and an inadequate education, too many of America's children risk falling behind in America's increasingly competitive knowledge based economy even before they reach puberty.

• Third, in the second and third decades of the twenty-first century, the outsized baby boomer generation born in the years after World War II will hit retirement age, which will put an enormous strain on all of society's institutions for relationships between the generations, including the Social Security and Medicare programs. The current intergenerational compact will not hold. The question is not whether change will occur, but only how and when.

These three long-term issues—continued productivity, inequality and opportunity, and the intergenerational compact—have been apparent to serious policy analysts for at least two decades. Yet year after year, America has only waved its hands at these problems and deferred systematic and substantial actions. This book lays out the problems and evaluates an agenda for action.

This book, a project of the Brookings Institution and the Urban Institute, with The American Assembly, was written by Rudolph G. Penner, senior fellow, the Urban Institute; Isabel V. Sawhill, senior fellow, the Brookings Institution; and Timothy Taylor, managing editor of *The Journal of Economic Perspectives*. This volume was prepared as background for an Assembly of forty-eight leaders from American business, law, media, nonprofit organizations, and academia that met at the Emory University Conference Center in Atlanta, June 10–13, 1999, under the auspices of Emory University, Morehouse College, and Spelman College. The final report of that meeting is included in an appendix.

Publication of this book and the Atlanta Assembly also launch a new multiyear series of The American Assembly titled "Uniting America—Toward Common Purpose." We chose the American economy as the starting point for the series because the issues

treated herein are fundamental to the other issues in the series and
to any hope for a more united America. A list of the Leadership
Advisory Group for the project is included in this volume.

The American Assembly is grateful to the following institutions
and individuals who provided funding specifically for this book and
project on the American economy:

- The Robert W. Woodruff Foundation
- Bradley Currey, Jr.
- The WEM Foundation
- Genuine Parts Company
- King and Spalding
- Sun Trust Bank, Inc.
- Wachovia Bank

In addition, The Assembly expresses its gratitude to those individuals and organizations who made contributions to the overall
Uniting America series. A portion of their support helped to create
this book and the corresponding Assembly:

- The Ford Foundation
- The Goizueta Foundation
- The Surdna Foundation
- The Coca-Cola Company
- The Xerox Corporation
- Walter & Elise Haas Fund
- Anonymous
- Eleanor Bernert Sheldon

As in all of our publications, the policy views expressed in this volume are those of its authors, and do not necessarily reflect the views
of The American Assembly, nor its co-sponsors or participants.

It is our hope and belief that this volume and the future Assemblies in the Uniting America series will help to stimulate a con-
structive national dialogue in the United States that will contribute
toward a more united America.

Daniel A. Sharp
President and CEO
The American Assembly

Updating America's

Social Contract

1

An Agenda for
the Radical Middle

The U.S. economy purred along like a well-oiled machine in the closing years of the 1990s. The economy expanded steadily since the trough of the previous recession in March 1991, making this economic expansion one of the longest in U.S. history. From 1997 through 1999, unemployment remained under 5 percent while inflation hovered at less than 2 percent. Unemployment had not been that low for three consecutive years since the late 1960s, and inflation had not been so subdued for three consecutive years since the early 1960s. The federal budget flip-flopped from deficit to surplus in 1998, leading to the first budget surplus since 1969. The budget surpluses are likely to last for at least several more years— a shocking possibility when you consider that the federal government has not had four or more consecutive years of budget surpluses since the 1920s.

When the economy performs well, the effects resonate throughout society. For example, the dry statistics of lower unemployment rates have real-life consequences for millions of workers and households for whom job opportunities have expanded and incomes are more secure. The lower inflation rate means that long-term planning, by households and businesses, can take place in a steady and predictable environment. The robust economy may have contributed to favorable social indicators as well. Crime rates have dropped sharply; the rate of teen pregnancies has declined; and in recent years, the poor are sharing to a greater extent in America's growing prosperity.

When a storm is raging, sometimes it is all one can do to plug the leaks and stay afloat. But when the weather is fair, it is time to mend sails, caulk the hull, and plan the next trip. Similarly, when the economy is in recession, or when unemployment and inflation are hitting high levels, sometimes it is all policy makers can do to address those immediate issues. However, when the economic climate is as favorable as it has been in recent years, there should be time and space to consider long-term issues that might otherwise be neglected.

We focus on three such long-term issues in this book. First, productivity growth has increased more slowly in recent decades than in some earlier eras, which has translated into slower improvements in the average family's income. Second, economic inequality has risen sharply since the late 1960s, and there is concern that the opportunities for those at the bottom to move up the economic ladder have become more limited. Third, the retirement of the baby boom generation in the opening decades of the twenty-first century will pose challenges for public policy and for society as a whole.

Each of these three issues has a strong economic component, but their resolution will require that the nation reach beyond purely economic considerations. These issues are all part of America's "social contract," a term that describes the explicit and implicit agreements among the members of a political community that define the rights and responsibilities of people vis-à-vis their government. Americans place a high value on allowing individuals to pursue their own happiness in their own way. However, collections of individuals with no common vision and no social mechanisms for dealing with problems affecting the whole can be highly vulnerable. The challenge is to find the right balance in the social contract between individual freedoms and what Americans must do as members of a community acting through and with the assistance of a democratically elected government.

Renegotiating the social contract is always difficult. Such renegotiations involve intertwined questions about who will bear the costs and who will receive the benefits, about the appropriate balance between individuals and their government, and about fundamental social values.

For example, in thinking about long-term productivity, issues arise of how much the present generation of Americans should worry about the standard of living that will be enjoyed by future generations, and thus how much the nation should seek to increase the level of saving and investment even if it means tightening belts and accepting a lower standard of living in the present. In thinking about issues of inequality and poverty, there are questions of how much America's more fortunate owe to the less fortunate, and the extent to which assistance should be structured to reflect the value that many people place on self-supporting work, stronger families, and individual responsibility. In considering the issues that will arise as America turns older, the current promises made by Medicare and Social Security will not be sustainable according to current projections of expected revenues and expected costs. In renegotiating America's intergenerational social contract, either younger generations will have to pay much higher taxes or older generations will have to accept much lower benefits during their retirement, or some combination of the two.

In addressing the issues of long-term productivity, inequality and opportunity, and the graying of America, the authors of this book offer the perspective of economists who are also radical middle-of-the-roaders. A wise economist named Victor Fuchs wrote a personal manifesto a few years ago in which he declared:

Politically I am a Radical Moderate. "Moderate" because I believe in the need for balance, both in the goals that we set and in the institutions that we nourish in order to pursue those goals. "Radical" because I believe that this position should be expressed as vigorously and as forcefully as extremists on the Right and Left push theirs.

As radical middle-of-the-roaders, we do not pretend to agree completely on a unique set of policy options; indeed, our internal discussions sometimes reflected the value differences found in society at large. However, we do agree on several fundamental themes, which shape the tone of our argument throughout this book.

We agree that facing these issues of long-term productivity, inequality and opportunity, and the aging of America will require choosing between difficult trade-offs and taking action. No magic fairy or free lunch or "new economy" is going to emerge and obviate the need for these tough choices.

We believe that America's political system is not performing as well as its economic system. In the 1990s, partisan tensions and distrust rose even more rapidly than the GDP. It seems extremely difficult to achieve a consensus in any policy area, and politicians of both parties often seem more interested in a symbolic victory, suitable for a quick mention on the evening news, rather than in working to find common ground on substantive issues.

Finally, we believe that the reasonable middle is often much larger in society as a whole than it may appear if one listens to speeches from the floor of Congress or to the baying and barking of the commentators on political-attack talk shows. We believe that the middle ground needs outspoken and visible advocates. This book does not provide a quick recipe for curing the nation's ills; indeed, radical moderates find it difficult to believe that any magic cure-all is possible. Instead, our goal is to explain what the policy options are and to provide an honest rendition of their advantages and disadvantages. However, being moderate need not mean being wishy-washy. In cases where the arguments and evidence seem persuasive, we will draw firm conclusions. In cases where reasonable people may differ on the evidence, or where difficult conflicts of values may arise, we will enunciate and evaluate the key arguments and leave the reader to lean in one direction or the other. In steering this course, we hope to provide ammunition to other radical middle-of-the-roaders, and perhaps even to make some converts to the belief that in good economic times these long-term issues are ripe for action.

The U.S. Economy of the 1990s:
A Look Back

Before plunging into the long-term issues of productivity, inequality and opportunity, and the aging of America, chapter 2 offers an orientation guide to the good economic news of the 1990s.

The Clinton administration took office in 1993 with a number of commitments: to reduce budget deficits; to maintain an open trading system; to reform health care; to end welfare; to provide additional assistance to the working poor; and to invest more in education, research, and public infrastructure. Chapter 2 reviews the administration's successes and failures in these areas and concludes that President Clinton made some good policy choices, but that he was also rather lucky. Just as the coach of a sports team probably tends to receive too much credit when a team performs well and too much blame when it hits a losing streak, the president of the United States tends to get the lion's share of blame when the economy goes poorly, as George Bush discovered in 1992, and a heady share of credit when it goes well, as Clinton's pollsters found late in the 1990s.

The role of the government, and the president in particular, in shaping the economy is doubtless overstated. The U.S. economy is primarily based on private decision making by households and firms. The Federal Reserve, which is not under the direct control of president or Congress, plays a substantial role. Moreover, the course of the 1990s economy was heavily shaped by events and decisions that predated the Clinton years. However, even if Clinton was lucky in inheriting a fundamentally sound economy, he deserves credit for many of his economic policies, including his contribution to turning the budget deficit to a surplus; his promotion of an open global trading system through support of the North American Free Trade Agreement (NAFTA) and the World Trade Organization (WTO); and his role in recasting the safety net in a way that rewards work and not welfare.

Will the "New Economy" Take Us Where We Want to Go?

The performance of the U.S. economy in the 1990s was strong enough to make a number of observers wonder if the country had begun to enter the promised land of a "new economy," in which the marvels of new information and communications technology, combined with the competitive pressures and opportunities of global markets, have opened up unprecedented opportunities for long-term growth with little fear of inflation or recession. However, this talk of a "new economy" scrambles together several subjects that are better kept apart.

The "new economy" forces of globalization and technology are clearly causing a reshaping of many companies and industries in the U.S. economy. They are also probably contributing to shifts in the wage structure that have tended to benefit high-skilled U.S. workers and to penalize low-skilled ones, as will be discussed in chapter 4. However, the evidence is much, much weaker that these forces have fundamentally altered the U.S. macroeconomy.

Chapter 3 begins by discussing the impact of the new economy forces of globalization and technology, and then unpacks the arguments over the impact of these forces on macroeconomic variables like productivity, unemployment, inflation, and the chance of recession. The official growth rate of productivity did not surge as much as most people believe in the 1990s, certainly not enough to mark a sea change in the economy. To be sure, the official measures of productivity have certain flaws and biases, but taking these issues into account does not alter the conclusion. The reasons for lower unemployment in the late 1990s had more to do with the flexibility of U.S. labor markets, and to some extent with the age distribution of the population, than with new technology. Inflation rates have stayed low in recent years because of the good offices of the Federal Reserve, as well as the falling prices of imported commodities and oil in the aftermath of the meltdown of the economies of East Asia in 1997 and 1998. Recessions do seem to be less frequent in recent decades, but that has more to do with sensible macroeconomic and banking regulation policies than with whiz-bang computers and information flows.

Whatever one's conclusions about whether the U.S. macroeconomy has already been transformed in some fundamental way, there is still merit in discussing the package of pro-growth policies that might increase long-term rates of economic growth. America's social contract concerning the desired path of future economic growth is, at best, fragmented and implicit. It has long been understood that a set of growth friendly public policies would include investments in physical capital, human capital, and technology, occurring in a framework of market oriented institutions. But these issues have typically been broached sporadically and one at a time rather than being discussed as interrelated elements of a cohesive strategy for faster long-term economic growth.

The potential gains to an average household from pro-growth policies are substantial. In 1997 the median income for a family was $44,600. If this income level were to increase at 1 percent per year (setting aside inflation), then it will reach $56,100 by 2020. If pro-growth policies could increase the rate of growth to just 1.5 percent per year, a gain of one-half of 1 percent each year, then the median family would instead have an annual income of $62,800 by 2020.

More rapid economic growth would also have broader political consequences. It is easier to renegotiate any element of the social contract in an economy that is growing rapidly than in one that is growing slowly, because a growing economy offers the prospect of more winners and fewer losers. Indeed, it is difficult to think of a better time for public policy initiatives than when the economy is booming and the budget is in surplus.

Inequality and Opportunity: Winners and Losers in the New Economy

The flexibility and ceaseless churning of the market are the dynamics that allow it to take advantage of new technology and global opportunities. But these same dynamics can be hard on individuals, who through no fault of their own may find that their skills are now outdated or their firm is facing heightened competition from domestic or foreign producers.

A market oriented economy will inevitably produce a certain degree of economic inequality. After all, if a system is to provide incentives for efficiency and effort, it cannot reward everyone equally. In addition, the choices that people make about marriage, childbearing, and household living arrangements, about personal investments in education and training, and about saving for the future will all affect their subsequent incomes. But even if a certain degree of inequality and insecurity is to be expected in a market economy, society may conclude that the degree of inequality or insecurity is greater than it needs to be, or that the number of people living in poverty is too high. In this case, the challenge is to construct policies that address these issues but do not overly undermine incentives to work or to exercise responsibility for one's own life. Such efforts need not be inconsistent with a well-functioning market economy; indeed, one can argue that a market economy can drive forward more quickly and smoothly if it is combined with a carefully constructed set of shock absorbers.

A renegotiation of America's social contract with the poor had already begun in the late 1990s. The welfare system was revised in 1996 under the philosophy that public assistance to the poor should be only temporary, and that all of the able-bodied poor, including the mothers of young children, have an obligation to try to help themselves if they are to receive public support. The welfare reform effort is generally off to a positive start, but the jury is still out on many details of how the new system is working, and how it will work when the next economic downturn arrives and jobs become scarce. Moreover, the welfare reform legislation has little to say about what should be done for the low-skilled workers who are working, or trying to work, but whose families remain below or barely above the poverty line. Nor does the welfare reform act, in and of itself, offer any guidance about how to ensure that children born into poverty have a fair opportunity to escape into a better life.

Chapter 4 discusses these issues. It begins by sketching how inequality and poverty in the United States have worsened since the late 1960s—although the last few years have produced some good news on both fronts. The evidence that workers face greater job insecurity than in the past is mixed at best. With respect to social mobility, the United States has made considerable long-term progress in insuring that opportunity exists for people to move up and down the economic ladder, whatever their race, gender, or family background. But problems remain. Most importantly, family structures are weaker than in the past, and schools are insufficiently strong to compensate for what children do not learn at home.

The chapter discusses the merits of a range of policies that have been advocated to help the poor, to redistribute income, to deal with job insecurity, and to build a society in which opportunities for success are more broadly distributed. It concludes by emphasizing the importance of providing more assistance to the working poor in the form of wage supplements, child care, and health care. It also points to the critical importance of good education at the preschool, primary, and secondary level as vehicles for insuring that children from less advantaged families have an opportunity to compete for the jobs that will be available in the future.

The Evolution of America's Intergenerational Compact

Demographic shifts are earthquakes under an economy; everything trembles and then must resettle into new patterns. The most important long-run demographic trend affecting the economy and government budgets is the continual increase in life expectancy. Superimposed on this long-run trend is the huge demographic shift that occurred when rising birth rates produced the "baby boomer" generation, those in the generation born from 1946, just after World War II, up to the early 1960s. The baby boom was followed by a "birth dearth," as fertility rates tumbled in the 1960s and have remained at lower levels since.

The boomer generation has played a major role in the stereotypical images of America over time. For example, when the boomers were young in the 1950s, it was a time when America was thought to be family oriented, full of stay-at-home moms who focused on family. As the boomers came to adulthood in the 1960s and early 1970s, rebellious young people shaped the political and cultural agenda in their opposition to the Vietnam War and their openness to sex, drugs, and rock and roll. As the boomers became parents in their own right, during the later 1970s and into the 1980s, America became more culturally and economically conservative. In the 1990s mid-career baby boomers made up an America heavily concerned about job security and stock market options. The front edge of the boomer generation, led by Bill Clinton who was born in 1946, will hit age sixty-five in 2010. The aging of this generation defines what is sometimes known as the graying of America.

Today one American in eight is over the age of sixty-five; by 2030, it will be one in five. This demographic shift will bring about profound shifts in the U.S. economy. For example, since the elderly tend to draw down their savings rather than building them up, the United States is likely to become a very low-saving economy in the early decades of the twenty-first century. From 2010 to 2030, the growing number of retirees will essentially counterbalance the number of new workers entering the labor force, so there will be little growth in the labor force. However, the active and healthy retirees of tomorrow will comprise a huge and talented pool of volunteer and part-time labor. Every institution of American society, from business to government, from education to health care to social services, will be forced to grapple with these changes.

On the public policy agenda, the largest issues involve how Social Security and Medicare, the major policy programs focused on the elderly, will adjust to the graying of America. The programs are fundamentally pay-as-you-go; that is, current workers pay for current retirees in the expectation that in turn, they will be supported as future retirees by the following generation of workers. But this intergenerational compact, in which each generation supports the retirement of its predecessors, will be thrown out of whack by the oversized retirement of the boomer generation.

In the late 1990s America was beginning to discuss how to renegotiate its social contract with retirees. Politicians only used to mention Social Security and Medicare reform in the privacy of their own homes. Reforming those programs was called the third rail of politics: touch them and you will die. But in the last few years, a courageous, if still small, band of politicians has begun to offer real reforms. At least so far, the prospective reformers have not suffered at the ballot box, indicating that at least some of the American people are ready to contemplate the alternatives they face. However, given the inexorable nature of the demographic forces involved, this debate is proceeding more slowly than it should.

Chapter 5 examines the demographic stresses that are unsettling America's intergenerational compact, including the retirement of the boomers, longer life expectancies, and changes in typical retirement ages. After offering some speculation on the challenges this change will pose for American society and for production in the private sector, the discussion then buckles down to cases and considers the options available for reforming Social Security, and to a lesser extent, Medicare. Too much of the public discussion on these issues is focused on accounting issues like the projected size of the Social Security and Medicare trust funds at various dates instead of considering which adjustments society should make in response to the graying of America. The necessary changes are likely to involve altering the incentives provided in the structure of Social Security, Medicare, and laws regarding taxes and pensions to encourage people to save more as individuals and to continue working later in life.

The challenges of slow productivity growth, inequality and opportunity, and the graying of America have been readily apparent for several decades now, for all who have been willing to see them. They are not problems that will be solved once and for all with a single piece of new legislation, nor by a single private sector initiative, but instead will need to be addressed by the sustained and combined efforts of government, market, and the broader institutions of civil society. The dawn of the twenty-first century appears to be an especially propitious time to take strong steps to address these issues because the overall state of the U.S. economy is so remarkably healthy. We hope the strength of the U.S. economy at the end of the 1990s does not serve as an excuse for complacency, but rather as a source of vitality and energy for society to address these issues.

2

The U.S. Economy
of the 1990s:
A Look Back

During Bill Clinton's 1992 campaign for the presidency against incumbent George Bush, Clinton's campaign advisers kept a sign in their office that read, "It's the economy, stupid." Whenever candidate Clinton was tempted to venture into the thickets of foreign policy or social issues or political philosophy, they instructed him to take a deep breath, remember the sign, and focus on the economy. This strategy worked better than almost anyone had expected, helping candidate Clinton unseat an incumbent president who, just eighteen months before election day, was riding sky-high in the opinion polls after the conclusion of the Gulf War with Iraq.

How bad was the economic situation that Bill Clinton inherited when he took office in January 1993? How has the shape of the economy altered during his presidency? How much credit can Clinton claim for the strength of the economy in the 1990s, and how much credit should go to other economic and political forces?

This chapter concludes that the Clinton administration deserves moderate credit for its 1993 deficit reduction plan, for its commitment to open global markets, and for its attempts to restructure the safety net in a way that rewards work rather than just handing out welfare. In other areas, such as health care reform, the administration fumbled badly. But in addition, Clinton was lucky. He entered office and immediately inherited a birthing recovery. He was fortunate to have Alan Greenspan at the Federal Reserve striking a careful balance between keeping the economy moving forward while preventing inflation. He benefited from his predecessors' efforts to deregulate the economy, to clean up the savings and loan crisis of the 1980s, and to negotiate a major deficit reduction package in 1990. In short, Clinton both benefited from and contributed to the long expansion of the 1990s during which private investment and the stock market exploded, job opportunities expanded, and even those at the bottom of the economic ladder began to improve their lot.

The Economy Clinton Inherited

In 1992 the U.S. economy was flapping like a fish on a dock. A recession had started in July 1990, and although later evidence would argue that the recession had bottomed out in March 1991, the stirrings of economic recovery were not broadly apparent by election day in November 1992. While most economic recoveries start with a burst of rapid growth, making it relatively easy to spot them in the data, the economic recovery that started in 1991 was sluggish—making it hard to be certain that the recession had indeed ended. Thus the official announcement that the recession had hit bottom in March 1991 didn't come until December 22, 1992, about six weeks after Bill Clinton had won the presidency.

The sluggishness of the early economic recovery was apparent in the job statistics. The unemployment rate rose from 5 percent in March 1989 to 7.7 percent by June 1992. While this unemployment rate didn't match the 9.7 percent unemployment rate during the deep recession of 1981–82, nor the 8.5 percent unemployment rate recorded during the recession of 1974–75, it was disturbing enough. Perhaps even more troubling was that overall employment growth in the U.S. economy went flat in the early 1990s; the U.S. economy had 118.8 million employed workers in 1990 and 118.5 million employed workers in 1992.

Other economic signals seemed to be flashing a warning yellow, too. The federal budget deficit in 1992, for example, hit $290 billion. To be sure, one could argue that certain one-time events had elevated the deficit, like paying off depositors in the bankrupt savings and loans after *that* fiasco of the 1980s. Or one could argue that if viewed as a share of the overall economy, the budget deficit of 1992 was 4.7 percent of GDP, which was lower than the deficits from 1983 to 1986 (for example, the 1983 deficit was 6.1 percent of GDP). In proportion to the economy, the 1992 deficit was also much, much smaller than the deficits of 20 percent of GDP and more that were racked up to finance the fighting of World War II. But in raw dollar terms, setting aside any adjustments for inflation or the deficit relative to the economy, the $290 billion deficit was the largest in U.S. history.

To be sure, the economy also had some quiet strengths in the early 1990s. Inflation had sparked in the late 1980s, flaring from 1.9 percent in 1986 to 5.4 percent by 1990. While an annual rate of 5.4 percent looked darned good compared with, say, the inflation rate of 13.5 percent experienced in 1980, it was still a relief to many to see that by 1992 inflation was back down to 3 percent and still falling.

The U.S. trade deficit had soared in the 1980s, moving from a slight surplus in 1981 to a deficit of $167 billion by 1987. In the early 1990s it had moved back almost to balance. But most economists do not mechanically identify trade deficits as bad news and trade surpluses (or balance) as good news. Instead, there is a broad recognition that trade imbalances, whether deficits or surpluses, happen because of two factors: expansions and contractions in the economy and the balance between a nation's domestic savings and its domestic investment. In the mid-1980s the U.S. trade deficit blossomed because the U.S. economy was expanding faster than economies elsewhere, which meant that it was drawing in imports faster than it could sell exports. In addition, the U.S. government ran huge budget deficits, which meant that instead of foreigners using their U.S. dollars to buy U.S. goods and services, they bought Treasury bonds instead. Many economists would have welcomed the lower trade deficits of the early 1990s if they had been caused by higher levels of U.S. savings, so that foreign capital was buying U.S. products instead of being invested in the U.S. economy, but that's not what happened. Instead, the trade deficit improved in the early 1990s because a sickly U.S. economy was drawing in fewer imports, and it was easier for U.S. firms to sell to growing economies elsewhere in the world.

These statistics can easily be viewed as part of a common picture. A primary reason for the recession of 1990–91 was that the Federal Reserve had been concerned about the spurt of inflation in the late 1980s, and had moved to choke off that inflation by raising its benchmark "federal funds" interest rate from 6.7 percent in 1987 to 9.2 percent by 1989. The higher interest rates discouraged borrowing, whether by business for investment or by consumers for goods like houses and cars. With less buying power in the economy, inflation indeed came down, but the economy tipped into recession. The economic slowdown meant that firms were less eager to hire, and unemployment rose. It also meant higher budget deficits, since recessions are a time of depressed income and corporate profits, and thus lower tax revenues, and also a time of increased need for welfare and other government safety net programs, and thus higher spending.

Recessions are bad news, even relatively mild recessions like the one of 1990–91. However, they do tend to pass with time and the application of sensible macroeconomic policy by Congress and the Federal Reserve. Fiscal policy, as a by-product of the automatic application of a progressive tax system and a safety net of government programs, will tend to swell budget deficits automatically in recession years—like the $290 billion deficit of 1992—and those large deficits help to cushion the drop off in demand. In theory, Congress could go further and actively stimulate the economy by reducing taxes or raising government spending in ways that encourage businesses and households to spend more, and, as we shall see, the Clinton administration came into office proposing such a stimulus package. However, experience with such active fiscal management of the economy has not been encouraging, in part because by the time the fiscal stimulus works through the political process, is signed into law, and then works through the economy, it often comes too late to be effective; indeed, it may even be counterproductive, having a destabilizing effect after a recovery is already well underway.

Monetary policy played a larger role than fiscal policy in reviving the economy in the early 1990s. The Federal Reserve, seeing that the battle to nip off inflation had been won, steadily reduced its benchmark "federal funds" interest rate from 9.2 percent in 1989 to just 3 percent by 1993. Just as higher interest rates had discouraged borrowing and slowed the economy, these lower rates stimulated borrowing and buying power in the economy, and helped pull it out of recession.

When Bill Clinton was sworn into office in January 1993, the immediate economic problems most in the public mind were slow growth and rising unemployment, with the huge federal deficit lagging not far behind. But alongside the rise and fall of the business cycle, Clinton also entered office facing some longer-term economic issues that went beyond the recent changes in job statistics or interest rates. Three of these economic problems, in particular, had been around in one form or another for at least a decade before the 1992 election: slow productivity growth, rising inequality and declining opportunity, and a weakening compact between generations. These three issues were introduced in the first chapter of this book and will be discussed one at a time in the next three chapters, so they need not be discussed at great length here. However, to set the stage for the later discussion, it is useful to note how they appeared in the early 1990s.

Low rates of productivity growth were not just a problem of the Bush administration; in fact, low rates of productivity growth had been a problem since around 1970. The annual rate of productivity growth (as measured by output per hour in the business sector) fell almost in half, dropping off from around 3 percent per year in the 1950s and 1960s to just 1.0 percent per year from 1973 until 1982, and the 1.7 percent per year from 1982 to the mid-1990s. Income inequality had been increasing since the late 1960s or early 1970s. With the retirement of the baby boom generation looming only a few decades in the future, a commission led by Alan Greenspan—before he took up his post at the Federal Reserve—recommended major Social Security reforms in 1983. However, by the early 1990s it was apparent that more had to be done. The benefit levels promised under current law would substantially exceed the resources of the system by around 2030.

The U.S. Economy at the
End of the Twentieth Century

As Bill Clinton moves toward the completion of his second term of office, the economic picture has brightened considerably. The economy has grown steadily without a recession since March 1991. During the lengthy economic upswing of the 1960s, the economy grew for 106 consecutive months from February 1961 to December 1969. Moreover, the economic upswing of the 1960s may have been artificially extended by the rise in military spending during the Vietnam War, which helped boost the economy toward the end of that time—and then helped to generate a burst of inflation in the late 1960s and early 1970s. If the economic expansion of the 1990s extends through January 2000, it will be longer than any economic expansion that the U.S. economy experienced in the twentieth century.

While the length of the 1990s upswing was exceptional, the speed of economic growth during the 1990s was quite average. Over the long term, from 1960 to 1998, including periods of both growth and recession, the rate of growth of GDP adjusted for inflation was about 3.4 percent per year, as illustrated in Figure 1. During the economic upswing of the 1990s, from 1991 through 1998, the annual rate of growth was 3.5 percent. Of course, the period from the 1960s through the 1990s covers a lot of terrain, so the comparison may not be entirely fair. For example, population and the labor force were growing more quickly in the 1960s than in the 1990s, which tends to push up the growth rate of the economy. However, even the productivity figures, which measure what the average working person contributes to the economy, although improved relative to the 1970s and 1980s, haven't yet broken any records. It's just possible, on the other hand, that the economy is on the cusp of a new era. When an economy is recovering from a recession, rapid rates of growth are to be expected, but once it reaches full employment, the rate of growth usually slows down to a steady pace of around 2 percent a year, or perhaps a little more. Yet rates of economic growth have been much higher than this since 1996, despite an economy that is operating near capacity. Real

GDP growth averaged 4.1 percent a year from 1996 to 1998, fueled primarily by a productivity growth rate of over 2.5 percent a year. The expansion of the 1990s shows no sign of petering out. However, no gentle twisting of the statistics can turn the overall upswing of the 1990s into a period of red-hot economic growth.

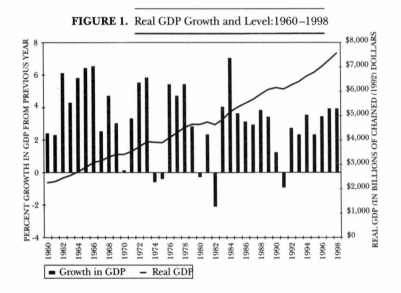

FIGURE 1. Real GDP Growth and Level: 1960–1998

Source: 1999. The Economic Report of the President. Table B-2.

As the economy has grown, the number of jobs has expanded dramatically and unemployment rates have correspondingly fallen. The employment figures have been one of the brightest spots of the Clinton administration's economic record. From 1992, the year before Clinton took office, to 1998, civilian employment in the U.S. economy rose from 118.5 million to 131.5 million—a rise of 13 million, or more than 2 million per year. Meanwhile, the unemployment rate, which had risen to 7.5 percent in 1992, had fallen to 4.9 percent in 1997 and just 4.5 percent in 1998. To many professional economists, such low rates of unemployment came as a genuine shock.

After all, unemployment rates hadn't consistently been below 5 percent since the late 1960s, as shown in Figure 2, and it was commonly believed that the government spending splurge on the Vietnam War had pushed unemployment rates to levels that were unsustainably low in the long run. America's rock-bottom unemployment rates look even better when compared to the unemployment rates experienced in many European countries, like Germany, Italy, and France, where unemployment rates approaching and exceeding 10 percent have now been the norm for more than two decades.

FIGURE 2. Unemployment Rate:1960–1998

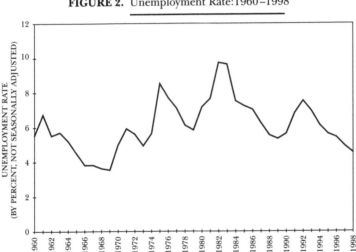

Source: 1999. Bureau of Labor Statistics (BLS).
Labor Force Statistics from the Current Population Survey.
From the BLS web site, accessed 5/1/99: http://stats.bls.gov/blshome.html

While the economy swelled and unemployment declined, inflation has stayed quiescent; in fact, it has actually declined. The inflation rate as measured by the Consumer Price Index (CPI) held at about 3 percent, or just a tad lower, from 1992 to 1996, before falling to 2.3 percent in 1997 and just 1.6 percent in 1998. This per-

formance was also astonishing to many economists; after all, inflation had not consistently been around 2 percent or lower since
nearly forty years ago in the early 1960s, as shown in Figure 3.

FIGURE 3. Change in the Consumer Price Index (CPI):1960–1998

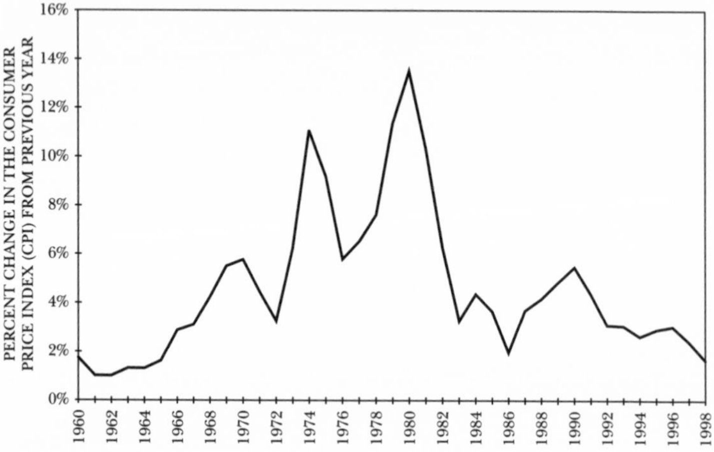

Source: Bureau of Labor Statistics. Consumer Price Index Data.
From the BLS web site, accessed 5/1/99: http://stats.bls.gov/blshome.html

The trade deficit reemerged with a vengeance in the late 1990s,
hitting an all-time record in 1998, and appearing likely to surpass
that record in 1999. This has provoked some public concern, since
many tend to see trade deficits as destroyers of American jobs and
as a sign that the U.S. economy is being treated unfairly by its trading partners. But given the strong growth in U.S. employment in the
1990s, and the steady growth of the U.S. economy, it is hard to
make the connection that the trade deficit is injurious to America's
economic health, at least in the short run. Remember, the primary
cause of the huge U.S. trade deficit in the late 1990s was that the
resurgent American economy was drawing in large quantities of
imports, while U.S. exporters, confronted with economic slowdowns

and recessions in the rest of the world, were having a hard time increasing sales. In the longer run, however, economists who are concerned about the trade deficit point out that it is a symptom of America's free-spending, low-saving ways. The U.S. economy is consuming more than it is producing, and the trade balance measures the surplus of those goods coming in over those going out. The U.S. economy is paying for this extra consumption by borrowing from abroad.

To be sure, borrowing from abroad is not necessarily a bad thing. As long as the inflow of foreign capital is sensibly invested in projects that have a long-term economic payoff, such loans can benefit both borrower and lender. But the capital-rich countries of the world have typically provided enough domestic savings to supply their own investment, while investing the rest in capital-poor countries around the world. The U.S. has reversed this pattern since the 1980s, drawing on capital from the poorer nations of the world to finance investment here.

This pattern of greater American reliance on inflows of foreign investment capital raises two concerns. One implication is that as the U.S. economy relies on foreign capital, a greater share of the return on American investment, like the interest payments on bonds and the gains from stock ownership, will also flow to those foreign investors. Moreover, a high level of foreign investment exposes the U.S. economy to the whims and vicissitudes of international capital markets. The United States is unusual among the nations of the world in that its economic prominence in the global economy means that most of its loans are denominated in its own currency. Other nations often owe money in U.S. dollars, rather than in their own currencies, which forces them to run the risk that if their exchange rate changes, obtaining those U.S. dollars to pay their debts may become expensive and difficult. Nevertheless, if at some point in the future foreigners lose confidence because they believe that the United States has been too profligate, they could reduce their holdings of U.S. dollar assets, thus causing turmoil in foreign exchange markets. At worst, if a loss of confidence in the U.S. economy were to occur, it could slash the available capital for investment in the U.S. economy. If the U.S. were to move toward a higher domestic savings rate, these dangers of reliance on foreign capital would be reduced.

There is one nagging fear about the economy that illustrates the well-known ability of economists to give even good news a worrisome tinge. The stock market has almost tripled during the Clinton years, with the Dow Jones Industrial Average, for example, rising from about 3,300 in 1992 to above 10,000 by early in 1999. This bull market wasn't new to the Clinton administration; it actually started in the 1980s. The Dow had also nearly tripled between 1983 and 1992, rising from 1,200 to 3,300 over those years. Of course, a rising stock market represents great gains in wealth for many private investors and pension funds, and has helped many companies raise funds for investment and expansion. Overall, the stock market boom has surely been a positive force for the economy.

But in the 1990s stocks have risen so far and so fast as to outstrip normal measuring sticks for valuation. For example, many investors look at the price-to-earnings ratio of stocks, or the P/E ratio, which is the total price of all the stock in the firm divided by the firm's annual earnings. Over the last century or so, stocks averaged a P/E ratio of about fourteen. Typically, a higher ratio meant that stocks were eventually headed for a fall, and a lower ratio meant they would at some point rise. By early in 1999, however, the P/E ratio for the broad range of stocks traded on the New York Stock Exchange was as high as twenty-five—an extremely high level by historical standards. Another measuring stick for stock market investors is to compare the "book value" of a company, which is determined by taking the value of all of a company's assets minus the value of its liabilities—with the stock price of the company. The stock market value of companies was typically about 200 percent of book value from the 1950s to the 1970s, then sagged to about 120 percent of book value in the early 1980s. However, by 1999 stock market value had risen to more than 500 percent of book value.

Stock market optimists argue that these sorts of stock valuation guidelines are outdated. Book value typically focuses on physical assets, rather than human or intellectual capital, so perhaps intangible assets have become more important in a way that book value doesn't capture. Perhaps firms are taking on more debt, which raises their interest payments but reduces their official "earnings," and thus makes P/E ratios look larger than they usually would.

At a more fundamental level, measuring sticks like P/E ratios are implicitly based on investors' perceptions of how much risk is involved, and thus how much the stock in a certain company is worth. Because of financial innovations like the widespread use of mutual funds and IRA and 401k retirement accounts, investors can invest in well-diversified portfolios of stocks while paying far lower commissions than in the past. This lowers the risks and the costs of investing in stocks, which also helps to explain why stock prices have risen so substantially. Indeed, it has been argued that financial markets have experienced a fundamental change, as investors have discovered that stocks are not as risky as they had thought and so are willing to pay more for stocks. Such fundamental shifts are not unknown; for example, in a reversal of historical patterns in the late 1950s, the dividend yield on stocks fell below the interest rate on bonds, where it has remained ever since. If such a shift in perceived risks has broadly occurred, then as long as investors remain comfortable with the associated risks, there is no reason to expect stock prices to decline, although the future rate of increase in stock prices may well be lower than it has been in the 1990s.

Or perhaps, just perhaps, the U.S. stock market is riding too high, the expectations of investors about future gains are overoptimistic, and the market is headed for a nasty fall. Alan Greenspan spoke famously in December 1996 about "irrational exuberance" in the stock market, and the stock market in mid-1999 was more than 50 percent higher than when he made that comment. A steep decline in the stock market, if that were to occur, would surely take some of the glow off the economy, although it would not necessarily lead to recession.

Finally, in an economic turnaround that still has Washington insiders reeling, the federal budget deficit has been converted into a surplus, which appears likely to continue for several years to come. As late as 1996 the mainstream budget projection was for deficits for years into the future. For example, the fiscal year 1996 budget that Clinton submitted to Congress projected that the deficit in the year 2000 would be $194 billion, almost the same as the $203 billion deficit actually experienced in 1994. However, by fiscal year 1998, the federal budget already had a surplus of $70 billion. Moreover, the 1999 projections of the nonpartisan Congressional Budget Office were for these surpluses to continue expanding through 2009.

CBO estimates that the budget surplus will be $111 billion in 1999, increasing to $383 billion in 2009, for a cumulative total of $2.7 trillion over the next ten years. However, these projected surpluses are predicated on a number of assumptions about the economy and about policy. In particular, if Congress should enact new tax cuts or spending increases, rather than paying down the past debt, then the future budget surpluses will be lower not only because of increased program outlays and lower revenues, but also because interest expenses on the debt will not fall as projected. Moreover, all budget projections have an element of uncertainty. Just as the budget surpluses appeared unexpectedly, for reasons that could only be analyzed after the fact, they could disappear unexpectedly, too.

All in all, the U.S. economy during the Clinton years has been a genuine success story: no recession, low unemployment, low inflation, a booming stock market, and a federal budget surplus. These accomplishments are real and notable and deserving of emphasis. But without taking anything away from the good news, there are also one new worry and three longer-term pieces of unfinished business that remain.

The new worry is the increased vulnerability of the U.S. economy to globalization and to events abroad. The U.S. economy has benefited from foreign trade in many ways: American consumers have been able, in effect, to shop the world for the best deals; American firms have found new markets for their goods and services; and the U.S. level of investment has benefited from the massive inflows of international capital. But while foreign trade is on the whole beneficial to the U.S. economy, that does not mean it is beneficial to each and every person. Even if more people gain from trade than lose from it, strong levels of trade and imports may cause a reshuffling of the U.S. economy, in ways that may contribute to greater wage inequality (a topic to which we return in chapter 4).

Both American jobs and financial institutions are now more dependent than ever on events outside U.S. borders. The potential risks of international involvement became especially apparent in 1997 when a banking crisis in Thailand set off a chain reaction that eventually spread across East Asia, and then to Russia, Latin America, and to some U.S. banks and investors, too. The existing international financial systems and institutions are not evolving quickly enough to match a world in which billions of dollars fly around the world at the stroke of a computer key. Although we do not address these issues in this book, we want to acknowledge their importance.

Instead, we will focus on the three nagging long-term issues we identified earlier: the prospect of a new economy and how to raise America's rate of productivity growth; the rise of inequality and concerns over opportunity in the U.S. economy; and how society will pay for the impending retirement of the baby boom generation. These problems have largely continued into the Clinton years, although some signs of progress were evident in the late 1990s. The rate of productivity growth, while slower in the 1990s than in the 1950s and 1960s, picked up and was especially strong at the end of the decade. Inequality of family incomes continued to increase during the early Clinton years, but stopped rising after 1993. Finally, the hard issues of how to deal with the eventual retirement of the baby boom were at least on the table for discussion, although they had not been dealt with in any substantial way through the later part of 1999.

How Much Credit Does Bill Clinton Deserve for the 1990s Economy?

The president of the United States, whoever he is, is often given too much credit when the economy goes well and too much blame when it goes badly. After all, the U.S. economy is made up of thousands of firms and millions of households. These economic actors are acting independently, buffeted by the pressure of events, competition, and new technologies. Neither the president nor Congress nor anyone else in the government controls their decisions in any direct way.

Moreover, when it comes to the federal budget or other legislation, the president must share power with Congress. Clinton faced a Republican controlled Congress after 1994, so the Republicans in Congress must share in the praise or blame for the laws that have passed since that time. When it comes to economic decision making, the president must also share power with the Federal Reserve, which has considerable latitude to set interest rates and regulate banks and other financial institutions as it sees fit.

The argument that a president has limited power over the economy cuts in two directions. On one hand, it would be peculiar to connect the president mindlessly to everything that happens in the economy, for better or worse, as if the president were a personification of GDP and unemployment statistics. On the other hand, the limited power of the president cannot exonerate him from responsibility, since even limited power can still be exercised for better or worse.

No president can be held accountable for the economic situation that he inherits. In terms of public perceptions, Clinton walked into a nearly ideal economic situation when he took office in January 1993. The recession had bottomed out in March 1991, and the economy had started to move forward. But given the lags in economic statistics and public perceptions, it appeared as if Clinton's mere arrival in office had brought about an economic recovery!

Moreover, when George Bush handed over the White House, he left a couple of gift-wrapped economic presents behind. One was legislation to clean up and pay off the savings and loan mess, which had plagued several regions of the U.S. economy. One reason the U.S. budget deficit was so high in the early 1990s, along with the impact of the recession in reducing taxes and raising spending, was that the federal government had insured the depositors in the many savings and loans that went bankrupt, and it needed to pay off those depositors. In fiscal 1991 alone, for example, the federal government spent about 1 percent of GDP in paying off the savings and loans. In addition, weaknesses of financial institutions like the savings and loans hindered regional economies by making it harder for local households and businesses to get credit.

An even larger gift was Bush's contribution to the Omnibus Budget Reconciliation Act of 1990, which tried to put the government on track toward a significant reduction in the budget deficit. Signing this act was one of the factors that cost Bush re-election. When Bush ran for the presidency in 1988, many in the Republican establishment viewed Bush as the sort of squishy and unreliable conservative who would allow new taxes. During his 1988 presidential campaign, Bush had sought to address their fears by emphatically declaiming: "Read my lips! No new taxes!" But Bush was sufficiently convinced of the need for a long-term strategy to reduce the budget deficit that in 1990 he signed on to a package of reforms in which he agreed to raise taxes in return for some Democratic support of spending caps. About 30 percent of the projected deficit reduction from the 1990 act was due to higher taxes. Most of the increase in taxes was focused on upper income taxpayers, but excise taxes also increased on gasoline, tobacco, and alcohol. On the spending side, the key element of the Bush deficit reduction package was to divide the budget into "mandatory" and "discretionary" categories. "Mandatory" spending covered programs like Social Security, where outlays are open-ended, depending only on benefit formulas interacting with demographic or economic trends. The rule here was "pay-as-you-go," that is, any increases in such spending (or any tax cuts, for that matter) could only be enacted if offsetting revenues or spending cuts were found elsewhere in the mandatory portion of the budget. For discretionary programs, legally binding spending caps were put in place. These budget rules were later extended after the Clinton administration took office and are an important reason for the fiscal discipline the federal government experienced during the decade of the 1990s.

As a candidate, Clinton proposed a wide range of policies. His 1992 campaign-trail book, *Putting People First*, written in short-snippet telegraphic style, has thirty-two chapters in 170 pages, and the chapters in turn are divided into numerous separate proposals. Many of these arguments were fleshed out and restated in the administration's first budget, released in February 1993, and in the first economic report of Clinton's Council of Economic Advisers, released in February 1994. To simplify the lengthy list of proposals from these documents, it's fair to say that Clinton emphasized a short-term stimulus package to boost the recovery, a longer-term set of public investments in lifelong education, research, and infrastructure, and a complementary effort to increase private investment by reducing the budget deficit. He argued that the rich had benefited more than the middle class from the economic upswing, and so the rich should pay a greater share of taxes. Clinton also promised to "end welfare as we know it," to support a North American Free Trade Agreement and an open global trading system, and to overhaul America's health care system to provide insurance coverage to all, while holding down costs.

However, when Clinton took office in 1993, and was faced with the task of putting together his first budget, he found that some of these priorities were potentially in conflict. For example, if he put more money into research, education and training, and infrastructure, the higher spending would make it harder to reduce the budget deficit. Moreover, a number of the president's closest economic advisers believed that one of his top priorities should be to reduce the budget deficit. Clinton came to agree with this view, and almost immediately after taking office in 1993, he proposed a deficit-cutting package that eventually became law as the Omnibus Budget Reconciliation Act of 1993. On the tax side, the biggest change was an income tax increase focused on the top 1.2 percent of households in the income distribution. The spending caps left behind by the Bush administration were extended; essentially, the overall discretionary portion of federal spending was to be frozen in nominal dollars, with no upward adjustments even for inflation, from 1993 to 1998. Despite the fact that the economy was recovering, Clinton still pushed a short-run stimulus package, but mercifully, the Congress voted it down.

Clinton had to fight hard for his deficit reduction bill, because a majority of Republicans were strongly opposed to raising taxes in any form—and a number of Democrats had qualms on the subject, too. The budget eventually passed without a single Republican vote in Congress. There was fear that the tax increases would happen immediately but the spending caps would not hold. That fear has turned out to be misplaced. In fiscal year 1992, just before Clinton took office, federal spending was 22.5 percent of GDP; by 1998 it was 19.7 percent of GDP, and according to projections by the nonpartisan Congressional Budget Office, federal spending will fall as low as 18.2 percent of GDP by 2002, assuming current laws remain unchanged and the spending caps continue to hold. The decline in spending would not have been possible were it not for the dissolution of the Soviet Union and the end of the cold war. Defense spending fell from 6.3 percent of GDP in 1986 to 3.1 percent in 1999. Nevertheless, nondefense discretionary spending, out of which most investments in the future—including investments in people—get made, has also been squeezed hard and is now as small relative to GDP as it was in the early

1960s before the War on Poverty and the expansion of numerous social programs began.

George Bush's 1990 deficit reduction deal and Bill Clinton's 1993 deficit reduction act, together with a smaller deficit reduction effort in 1997, have all helped to set the stage for today's budget surpluses. Of the three packages, Bush's was the largest (involving deficit reduction of $580 billion over five years, measured in 1997 dollars), while Clinton's 1993 effort was a close second ($474 billion). The 1997 bipartisan agreement was relatively small ($118 billion). But these budget acts alone are not the whole story. The big change in the budget picture has not come from deficit reduction legislation, but rather from the growing economy and stock market, which have pushed up tax revenues much higher than had been expected just a few years ago. From 1994 to 1999, federal tax revenues increased at an average rate of 8.3 percent per year, far faster than growth in the economy.

As a result of the rapid growth of the economy and the stock market, federal tax revenue will have risen from 18.4 percent of GDP in 1994 to an expected 20.7 percent of GDP in 1999. This level of taxes as a share of the economy is as high as America has ever seen in peacetime; indeed, it has been exceeded during only one year in U.S. history—in 1944, when taxes were high to finance fighting World War II. On the other hand, the tax take is high because of good economic news: stocks are soaring and incomes are up, especially among high earners. The higher level of overall tax revenue is not because tax burdens for most individual families have increased. A study by the Congressional Budget Office showed that tax burdens for families in the bottom 80 percent of the income distribution were either lower or about the same in 1999 than they were in any year back to 1977 (which is as far back as the study goes). Only the top 20 percent of all families are paying higher taxes as a percentage of their incomes. Despite the bigger tax bite, this group has done exceedingly well, with after-tax incomes that have increased 15 percent faster than inflation since 1985. These facts may help to explain why it was politically difficult to muster strong movement for tax cuts in the late 1990s, despite the relatively high tax take by the federal government.

The movement from budget deficits to budget surpluses has

helped to create a higher level of private investment. Fiscal discipline has meant that the federal government is no longer soaking up several hundred billion dollars each year to finance budget deficits, and these funds are now available to the private sector. With the threat of inflation low, the Federal Reserve has also been able to keep interest rates low, which has encouraged private investment, too. The economic recovery of the 1990s has been heavily driven by private investment. In the other economic expansions since World War II, business fixed investment accounted for about 15 percent of the growth during the expansion. In the expansion of the 1990s, business investment has accounted for about 25 percent of the growth.

Along with the 1993 budget deal, Clinton can claim some other economic successes. Clinton's proposed health care reform crashed and burned before a skeptical Congress in 1994. However, he fulfilled his promise "to end welfare as we know it" with the passage of the Personal Responsibility and Work Opportunity Reconciliation Act of 1996, more commonly referred to as the welfare reform act. Equally important, if less well known, was the enactment of a major expansion of the Earned Income Tax Credit (EITC) in 1993 that provides as much as $3,700 a year in cash assistance to working poor families with children. Welfare reform in combination with the EITC expansion has shifted the way in which America deals with its poor toward a much greater emphasis on requiring and rewarding work. We will set the topic of welfare reform aside here, and then take it up again in the chapter 4 discussion of inequality and opportunity.

Clinton has also taken several strong steps toward global free trade, including the signing of the North American Free Trade Agreement with Mexico and Canada and completing the Uruguay Round of trade talks that led to the formation of the World Trade Organization, which replaced the General Agreement on Tariffs and Trade (GATT). In the end, from the standpoint of the United States, NAFTA was probably more about the symbolism of free trade than its substance. After all, the economy of Mexico is barely 5 percent of the United States—or to put it another way, the GDP of Mexico is about the size of the greater Los Angeles metropolitan area. The mainstream economic estimates of the likely effect of

NAFTA, which were often drowned out by those with dire predictions of disaster or dramatic predictions of success, were that it would increase U.S. output and employment by one- or two-tenths of a percent in the short run, which is an amount barely noticeable in the context of the overall U.S. economy. (The expected positive consequences were considerably larger for Mexico, however, and in the areas of the United States that border on Mexico, the effects are much more noticeable.) The establishment of the World Trade Organization is potentially of greater long-term importance as an institutional tool for reducing trade barriers around the world and leading to greater free trade, but much depends on whether the United States takes a strong position of leadership toward free trade within the organization.

At the end of the 1990s it seemed unclear whether the United States would take such a position. A majority of congressional Democrats opposed Clinton on both NAFTA and WTO; in recent years, a number of Republicans have begun to express doubts as well. In fact, when a January 1999 survey asked Americans, "Is protectionism or free trade best for your own country's prosperity?" protectionists outnumbered free traders by 56 percent to 37 percent. Protectionists like Pat Buchanan on the far right or Ralph Nader on the far left find a ready audience. The fact that America's trade deficit is enormous and growing will also exert political pressure against free trade, even though the trade deficit of the late 1990s was basically a consequence of America's booming economy. Some advocates of free trade fear that the Clinton administration has become half-hearted in its support of free trade, and that the rhetoric of the administration has been shifting more toward talk of retaliation against "unfair" imports rather than opening markets further.

Clinton's successes in the areas of welfare reform and free trade would not have been possible without Republican support. Congressional Democrats opposed both initiatives. In judging Clinton's economic record, it is thus intriguing that on budget policy he depended on support from his party, but on other issues, he has often depended on building coalitions with the opposing party.

When it comes to sharing power for economic decision making, Clinton owes a considerable debt of gratitude to one person: Alan Greenspan at the Federal Reserve. It's worth remembering that

Greenspan was originally a Republican appointee, and a former head of the Council of Economic Advisers during the Ford administration, so there is no particular reason to suppose that Greenspan set out to help Clinton politically. But as it turns out, Greenspan has helped a great deal to make the Clinton economic record look good.

As pointed out earlier, the Fed's efforts to choke off inflation in the later 1980s helped to bring on the recession of 1990–91, the albatross around Bush's neck as he ran for re-election. The Fed's efforts to lift the economy out of that recession with lower interest rates bore fruit just as Clinton took office. In early 1994, in the midst of Clinton's first term, Greenspan became concerned that inflation was about to get started again, and in a highly controversial move, the Fed raised its benchmark federal funds interest rate from 3 percent in January 1994 to 6 percent by April 1995. There was a considerable outcry at the time, although it isn't easy to remember it now, that the Fed was choking off the economy because it feared the mere shadow of inflation, not even the reality. But then the Fed started cutting interest rates again, and the combination of lower interest rates, along with the confidence that inflation was well under control, helped to boost the economy and the stock market in time for Clinton's 1996 election campaign against Bob Dole, and during Clinton's second term as well.

Clinton and his economic team have strictly refrained from criticizing the Fed. Of course, with the economy going well, there hasn't been much to criticize. But even when interest rates were rising in 1994, and some Democratic partisans were panicked that Greenspan, that Republican at the Fed, would capsize the presidency of Democrat Clinton, the White House team simply made general statements in support of the goal of low inflation, and stayed out of the way. This silence showed a considerable political maturity. The Federal Reserve is technically an independent agency, but if it comes under heavy political pressure, it sometimes feels the need to bend to that pressure. The Clinton administration contributed to the credibility and authority of the Fed, and thus to the goal of keeping inflation low in the longer term, by being supportive of the Fed and the goal of low inflation even when such support did not necessarily appear in its own short-term interests.

In terms of economic policy, Bill Clinton has been both good and lucky. In particular, he deserves credit for the 1993 deficit reduction plan; for keeping a fairly hard line against spending increases during the years since 1993; for his welfare reform bill; for his (moderate) support of free trade. But Clinton was also lucky in that he entered office at the beginning of a long recovery; because the explosion of the stock market has helped raise tax revenues; and because he has had the good luck to have Alan Greenspan's steady hand at the Federal Reserve. He was also lucky to be elected president of a fairly well-functioning economy where deregulation had already taken place in a number of industries, where the financial problems of the savings and loans and banks in the 1980s had already largely been cleaned up, and where wave upon wave of innovation in information and communication technologies were transforming the economy. Perhaps most of all, Clinton was lucky to be elected president of a nation with a free press, a functioning legal system, active nonprofit institutions like churches, universities, and hospitals, and a tradition of flexibility and change in the context of a market economy. In giving credit for economic performance, it must always be remembered that the U.S. economy doesn't happen in a vacuum, but rather against a greater backdrop of a well-functioning civil society—and no president can claim much credit for the creation of these broader institutions.

3

Will the "New Economy" Take Us Where We Want to Go?

The economic upswing of the 1990s had some intriguing and unexpected traits. Most economic expansions start quickly as the economy snaps out of recession and then level out over time. At some point, a combination of adverse economic events and corresponding reactions—or overreactions—by the Federal Reserve in its interest rate policies can slow the economy, or even topple it into recession. However, the economic expansion of the 1990s did not ignite quickly and then gradually moderate. It began with slower-than-average growth, with the economy growing in real terms by only a modest 3.3 percent in 1992 and 2.4 percent in 1993. More recently, the growth in real GDP has been 3.7 percent in 1996, 4.5 percent in 1997, and 4.3 percent in 1998. Apparently, the expansion of the 1990s is one with a strong second wind!

During the economic upswing of the 1990s, unemployment fell dramatically while inflation remained quiescent. The unemployment rate for 1998 was 4.5 percent, marking the first time in nearly three decades that unemployment had been less than 5 percent for two consecutive years. Inflation sunk to 1.6 percent in 1998, the lowest since that that rate was matched in 1965. The Federal Reserve has had little cause to worry overmuch about raising interest rates to fight inflation. In fact, the Fed felt confident enough that inflation was not a primary concern that it was willing to reduce its benchmark federal interest rate from 5.5 percent in September 1998 to 4.75 percent by December 1998 in an effort to build investor confidence in a global economy that had been shaken by threats of debt defaults and market meltdowns in Russia, Brazil, and East Asia—although this decrease in interest rates was rolled back when the Fed raised its benchmark interest rate several times in the second half of 1999.

Thus the growth upswing of the 1990s offered a special combination of strengths: a lengthy recovery, a growth rate that seems to be strengthening rather than moderating, continued job growth, and dwindling inflation. This remarkable performance has caused some to wonder whether the U.S. economy has gone through a fundamental structural transformation to a situation where more rapid growth without risk of inflation will continue for the foreseeable future, barring grievous errors of macroeconomic policy by the government.

This chapter asks whether the current economic expansion signals the beginning of a new economic world, spurred on by innovations in computing and communications—a world where the business cycle has been abolished, productivity has been permanently increased, and inflation is no longer a threat. Certainly, the economy appears to be more stable than it used to be. In the period since World War II, economic expansions have become longer than in earlier times. Also, the lack of inflation in the face of low unemployment has surprised many economists, even though similar good news was experienced for some years in the early and mid-1960s. But the real puzzle is productivity growth. Anecdotes abound about the application of exciting new technologies and about cost-saving innovations in individual firms. But no extraordinary resurgence of productivity growth is apparent in official economic data. Of course, the official data are imperfect, and measures of productivity growth are undoubtedly biased downward. But these imperfections and biases have existed for a long time. To argue that a new economy has arrived, it must be shown that those biases have been growing over time—and thus that actual productivity growth exceeds the officially measured levels by substantially more than in the past—and that case is much harder to make. Indeed, the reverse is more likely, because government statistical agencies have been working to reduce biases in the measurement of productivity, and the most important corrections have tended to move measured productivity upward.

Whether or not a new economy has arrived, certain old familiar policy measures can still benefit the economy. Preserving the budget surplus from both the tax cutters and spending boosters can add to domestic saving and investment. Improving education and persuading people to work longer can enhance the supply of human capital and the productivity of labor. Targeted tax incentives for saving and investing may also make sense, although these steps are much more controversial since reducing the number of tax incentives sprinkled throughout the tax code, and instead having lower tax rates overall, may create a better environment for long-term productivity growth. Other policies that may encourage productivity growth involve research and development, antitrust policy, and government investment in infrastructure. All are examined in more detail in what follows.

The Drivers of the New Economy: Globalization and New Technology

Those who argue for the existence of a "new economy" of rapid, recession-free growth typically point to two main forces that, in their view, have fundamentally changed the economy: the forces of globalization and new technology.

The U.S. economy has clearly become more intertwined with the global economy in recent decades. In 1970, for example, imports were 5.3 percent of the U.S. GDP; in 1997 imports were 13 percent of GDP. Thus the share of imports relative to the U.S. economy has more than doubled in the last few decades. This shift is clearly substantial, but it's also worth keeping in perspective.

Most of the U.S. economy is not directly involved with trade and does not even compete directly with imported products. Much of the service sector of the economy is not especially competitive with foreign products at all. When buying a house or getting a haircut or attending a football game or going out to dinner, the service you are buying can't be imported from Japan or Germany or Korea or Mexico. Moreover, many countries around the world find that foreign trade plays a far, far larger role in their economies than it does in the United States. Smaller countries, and those bordered by many trading partners rather than by two wide oceans (as is the United States), often have quite a large share of imports to GDP. For example, in Belgium, a small nation surrounded by European trading partners, imports are 63 percent of GDP. Finally, the shift toward globalization has clearly been going on for several decades, not just in the 1990s, so any effects from the shift should be perceptible over time, not just in recent years.

A rise in foreign trade should affect an economy in a number of ways. Foreign trade means that U.S. consumers have the ability to buy from anywhere in the world. In turn, this creates competitive pressure on U.S. firms to hold down prices, to raise quality, and to reduce their costs—in part, by holding down wage increases for U.S. workers. Business costs can also be restrained by importing less expensive supplies of physical materials and inputs from abroad. An expansion of trade opens up new markets to U.S. producers. In a global economy, producers are selling everywhere in the world, not just in their home market, so they are less vulnerable (although not invulnerable!) to a downturn in their home market. It also means that more U.S. producers are exposed to a wider range of competition, which should spur firms to greater efforts at innovation and competitiveness. Taking advantage of selling in the larger globalized market may also allow some firms to take advantage of economies of scale, that is, to lower their average cost of production as their level of output increases.

New technology, meaning especially the new information and telecommunications technologies, is the other driving force behind theories of the "new economy." It's hard to obtain precise estimates of the impact of computers on the economy (a point to which we will return), but the fact that computers have become more widespread doesn't seem in doubt. The direct production of computers has become a major industry; in 1996 the value of shipments of computers and office equipment reached more than $100 billion per year. But of course, the main changes wrought by the new information technology do not reside within the industry itself, but rather are located in the application of new production techniques among users of this technology and the creation of new products and services for consumers. As recently as 1980, relatively few homes or students had easy access to a personal computer; in 1997 35 percent of all U.S. households had a personal computer, and 10 percent reported that they use it sixteen hours or more each week. Thanks to digital technologies, students graduating from college in the next few years may never have seen a typewriter or an old-style long-playing record. In the business sector, real spending on computers was twelve times as large at the end of the 1990s as at the end of the 1980s.

Computing power has become ubiquitous in the business world, transforming one industry after another. Some of the changes are obvious to consumers, like automatic teller machines in the banking industry or the use of bar codes in supermarkets. Many other changes are less obvious, like allowing newspapers to be laid out on a computer screen before being printed; or transforming the business of travel agents and vacation destinations; or tying together sales, production, accounting, and tax records; or the control of robots in manufacturing plants. In recent years, prices of business computers and peripheral equipment fell by about 25 percent in 1996, 25 percent more in 1997, and again in 1998, as machines that could do more and more cost less and less. The changes and innovations seem likely to keep coming. The number of master's and doctoral degrees given each year in computer and information sciences rose from 1,600 in 1970 to 10,300 in 1995.

The special wonder of the new computer and telecommunications technologies is that they apply to so many industries in so many different and unexpected ways. They are generic technologies of transformation, capable of finding application everywhere. As one example (from Nathan Rosenberg of Stanford University), consider how computers have helped productivity in the airline industry.

At first glance, one might think that the impact would be minimal; certainly, when IBM was manufacturing early computers back in the 1950s, few commentators foresaw any particular reason why these immense adding machines should have any particular impact on airplanes. However, sophisticated computers have allowed fundamental aerodynamic research on the shape of planes, since many designs could be tested and modified on the computer rather than needing to build costly prototypes and test them in wind tunnels. These advances have had a substantial impact on fuel efficiency. Computers help run the instrumentation in the cockpit, to the extent that the phrase "automatic pilot" has become part of the common vocabulary. The combination of computers and weather satellites helps determine the best flight paths, which may save $1 billion worth of fuel a year. Tickets and seating arrangements, as well as the internal accounting and bookkeeping of the airlines, are all handled by computers. Computers are used for the simulators that teach pilots to fly and allow ongoing retraining. Computers, together with radar, handle air traffic control.

This example of the protean power of computers and communication technologies could be multiplied across the economy a thousand-fold and more, from services to manufacturing industries, from mom-and-pop operations to transglobal firms.

A wave of powerful new technology should have several effects on the economy. It should raise productivity growth. Higher productivity should also mean higher wages, at least for those who use these technologies in their day-to-day work. By holding down costs, computers may also help to keep inflation in check. The combination of computers and telecommunications growth also heats up the degree of competition in the economy and thus may encourage still further technological growth and development.

The driving forces of the "new economy," globalization and technology, career along hand in hand. One of the reasons why foreign trade can expand so strongly is that communication around the world and managing many far-flung operations around the world have become easier. The new technologies also give those nations who use them a different set of production capabilities, which in turn encourages trade with nations that have not yet developed such capabilities. As one example, consider a company like Nike, which in the mid-1990s had 2,500 U.S. employees, but drew on an indirect workforce of perhaps 75,000 workers scattered across Asia. Without computer and communications technologies, that sort of globalized firm would be much more difficult, if not impossible, to operate.

The Weak Macroeconomic Implications of the New Economy

There is no doubt that globalization and technology are economic forces of extraordinary importance, which are transforming large parts of the economy. Indeed, in chapter 4 we will argue that these forces have affected the inequality of wages in the U.S. labor market, and perhaps also the degree of job security. However, even though the forces of the "new economy" have altered the shape of the economy in certain ways, the evidence is actually quite weak that the "new economy" forces of globalization and new technology have caused a substantial transformation in productivity growth, inflation, unemployment, or the chance of recession. Let us consider each of these possible connections in turn.

Productivity and the New Economy

The major difficulty in arguing that the forces of the "new economy" have raised productivity is that the data, until very recently, didn't actually show that productivity has risen. One straightforward way of measuring productivity growth is to look at output per hour of persons in the business sector—a statistic compiled by the Bureau of Labor Statistics (BLS). This measure of productivity rose at an average rate of 2.0 percent per year from 1960 to 1998, a time period covering several recessions and economic upswings. If one looks only at the uninterrupted period of economic growth from 1991 to 1998, one sees that with the benefits of globalization and technology, the rise in productivity was (wait for it!) 2.0 percent per year. The annual change in labor productivity in the business sector is shown in Figure 4. Although the productivity figures bounce up and down from year to year, with a stabilizing eye one can see the lower levels of productivity in the 1970s and the gentle resurgence in productivity since then. But this hardly has the appearance of a growth miracle, especially since the time period from 1991 to 1998 does not involve any recessions. In fact, productivity growth since 1991 does not look better than the performance for other long economic upswings, like those in the 1960s and the

1980s. Confronted with this extremely average performance of the productivity statistics in the 1990s, academic economists often cite a wry comment attributed to Nobel laureate economist Robert Solow of MIT: "We see the computer revolution everywhere except in the productivity statistics."

FIGURE 4. Annual Change in Labor Productivity in the Business Sector: 1960–1998

Source: 1999. Bureau of Labor Statistics (BLS). Quarterly Labor Productivity Data. Extracted from the BLS web site, 5/3/99: http://stats.bls.gov/lprhome.htm

Advocates of the "new economy" perspective tend to become impatient when confronted by these dry statistics on productivity and growth. Sure, they admit the raw statistics. Who can deny them? But they point out that even the official data show a rise in productivity in the last few years. Productivity growth was 2.7 percent in 1996, 1.9 percent in 1997, and 2.8 percent in 1998. Moreover, the proponents of the new economy then go a step further to argue that productivity and economic growth are actually increasing faster than is being measured by the government statistics. To understand this criticism, it's necessary to take a brief digression into how the government calculates productivity changes. Basically, there are three steps: calculating the amount of output produced in each year, adjusting for inflation so that only the real increase in output is measured, and then dividing by an input, like hours worked.

The chief measure of national output is gross domestic product, which is estimated by statisticians at the Bureau of Economic Analysis (BEA) in the U.S. Department of Commerce. Their task is not an enviable one. No single survey of the entire economy exists, so they incorporate and weave together results from many different surveys, including those done by other branches of government, like the Census Bureau, the Department of Transportation, the Health Care Finance Administration, and the Department of Agriculture. They also rely on a variety of foreign trade statistics and statistics from state and local government. All of these sources, and the methods for combining them, are continually being updated and revised. Clearly, the calculation of GDP is not a finely calibrated measurement, like something out of a physics laboratory. In particular, measures of very short-term movements of GDP are clearly unreliable. However, as time passes and the government statisticians work out the kinks in their data and methods, the GDP data do a fair job in measuring longer-term trends.

The real argument over productivity lies with the inflation statistics. The estimates of GDP measure the economy in *nominal* terms, that is, they measure the dollar volume of what is bought and sold, but they do not distinguish as to whether changes are due to inflation in prices or to real growth in the economy. Thus to figure out growth in real GDP, one must take the estimate of nominal GDP and adjust for inflation. Say that the GDP grows by 5 percent in a year, but the measure of inflation is 2.8 percent. Then the real growth in the economy would be the remaining 2.2 percent.

The most-cited measure of inflation is the Consumer Price Index. In constructing the CPI, the BLS collects prices on about 71,000 different items either each month or every other month, at about 22,000 different retail outlets. It also collects data on rental prices from about 35,000 housing units. Of course, the BLS must sample the goods that people actually buy, at the outlets where they actually shop, so surveys are done to make sure that the selection of goods and outlets is representative. New goods and shopping outlets are rotated into the sample on an ongoing basis.

To construct an overall measure of inflation for purposes of measuring the real change in output, one has to go past the consumer goods included in the CPI and also estimate inflation measures for investment goods, and exports and imports as well. Components of the CPI are used to construct approximately 57 percent of the business output measure that is used by the Bureau of Labor Statistics to compute productivity figures. Broadly similar problems arise in all attempts to measure inflation rates regardless of the good or service being studied. U.S. government statisticians make a conscientious effort to resolve such problems; indeed, the quality of U.S. statistics is far better than in most other countries around the world. Yet any approach to calculating inflation, in the consumer sector or in other sectors, is subject to two broad critiques.

First, there is a problem of substitution. As the price of a good or service rises, the laws of supply and demand suggest that people are likely to consume less of it. As the price of something falls, conversely, people are likely to consume more. In turn, this means that goods whose prices are rising should receive slightly less weight over time in calculating the inflation rate for the overall economy, while goods whose prices are falling should receive slightly more weight. But how much should the weights change? Answering this question separately for each of the tens of thousands of products in the inflation surveys would be a difficult statistical task, and so the challenge has been to come up with a broad rule that generally captures the average amount of substitution that occurs. Several changes have been made in recent years that take substitution into account to a greater extent, and the BLS has announced that it will be adopting a new weighting system for the CPI in the future. But the problem is not an easy one to solve completely.

The second problem is the issue of quality and new goods. In the area of medical services, for example, the rising price of a day in a hospital room partly reflects raw inflation—that is, a higher price for the same good—and partly reflects an improvement in quality—that is, paying more because patients are getting more. A true measure of inflation would subtract out the increase in quality, but measuring quality is a difficult business. The new goods problem is a relative of the quality problem. The quality of telephone services increased substantially when a new good—say, the mobile, wireless phone—became widely available, but it took several years before the price of that new good was fully rotated into the official calculation of inflation. New goods are rotated into the index gradually, and the process is now being speeded up. But as with the substitution problem, it is doubtful that the new goods or quality problem will ever be solved completely.

Issues of quality and new goods abound in the U.S. economy: the invention of the automatic teller machine affects the quality of banking services; the invention of the VCR affects the quality of home entertainment; and so on. While most of the observed quality changes are probably positive, it's important to remember that not all are positive. Not that long ago, for example, most gas stations had employees who would pump your gas and check the oil and tire pressure. Yes, self-service gasoline costs less, and its popularity shows that many people are willing to pump their own gas in exchange for the lower price. Nonetheless, part of the lower price for self-service gasoline is due to a diminished quality of service, not just to a raw change in the price of gasoline.

If the inflation rate is overstated because it does not fully take substitution and issues of quality and new goods into account, then estimates of the growth of the real economy are understated. When *real* output is divided by hours worked, to generate an estimate of productivity, the productivity gain will also be understated. As a result, economic welfare is rising more quickly than the official statistics show. However, two substantial difficulties arise in attempting to argue that this mismeasurement of inflation is causing government statistics to misread an extraordinary recent surge of real productivity growth.

The first problem is that the arguments about an upward bias in the inflation rate, and the corresponding downward bias in the rate of productivity growth, have been well known to economists for decades; in fact, a prestigious commission of economists pointed out these very issues in a 1961 report to the Bureau of Labor Statistics—

and the academic literature on the point has still earlier roots. If the bias has been roughly constant over time, then measured statistics have consistently understated the *level* of real living standards and the *level* of productivity, but should not have affected their rates of growth. There can only have been a hidden surge in productivity growth recently if the measurement bias has suddenly grown, and it is difficult to see why that would have occurred.

The second problem with the mismeasurement thesis is its failure to recognize recent changes in the way the government calculates inflation. As noted above, the BLS has recently been working hard to reduce upward biases in measures of inflation. In 1996 a prestigious panel of economists chaired by Michael Boskin of Stanford University highlighted the relevant issues and offered an estimate that the official annual rate of inflation measured by the Consumer Price Index was overstated by 1.1 percent, thus leading to an annual underestimate of about the same amount of real economic growth. Some government statisticians at the BLS thought that the Boskin report may have overstated the bias, but the report nonetheless served a useful purpose. Government statisticians had been working on methods to reduce biases for years, and the report gave them political cover for putting some of their findings into effect. By early 1999 nonpartisan sources like the Congressional Budget Office estimated that by rotating new goods into the sample more quickly and making various adjustments in its calculations to account for substitution of goods, the BLS has already eliminated about half of the problem identified by the Boskin Commission report, and further corrections are underway.

The fact that the inflation statistics are now being calculated in a subtly different way, in a way that makes inflation look smaller and economic growth look bigger by about 0.5 percent per year, puts some of the recent economic statistics in a new light. If one adds 0.5 percent to the measured inflation rate each year in the late 1990s, it still looks low, but not quite so rock-bottom. If one subtracts 0.5 percent per year from the encouraging productivity statistics for 1996–98, then the productivity performance of those years looks very ordinary indeed.

Economists have searched for explanations as to why the productivity gains from computers and new technology seem to be so much less than might have been expected and have offered three arguments. First, despite all the recent investment in computers by business, computers still represent less than 5 percent of the total stock of equipment and less than 2 percent of nonresidential fixed capital, which includes structures. If one looks around industrial America, there are still a huge number of machines and engines and forges and equipment that are not computers. Expecting the computer tail to wag the equipment dog may be asking too much.

Second, computers may have certain productivity-reducing effects. They may help the average employee save an hour per day— but that average employee may then spend that hour playing Solitaire, forwarding jokes by e-mail to friends, and surfing websites for future vacation destinations. The gains from computer productivity might also be offset to some extent by having the entire office immobilized for an afternoon when the system crashes, or by time taken up in learning new software, and paying computer gurus to tend the system. A variety of economic studies have looked at the experience of individual companies that made large investments in computers and commonly find that small or nonexistent productivity gains resulted.

A third argument for why few gains in productivity have been found so far is more optimistic about the future. This argument holds that new technologies, like the combination of computers and telecommunications, may take several decades to diffuse through an economy. A historical example (first cited in this context by Paul David of Stanford and Oxford Universities) is the electrical dynamo. The dynamo was invented late in the nineteenth century. However, it was not used on a wide scale, for lighting a city, until the Paris World Fair of 1900. At this point, although the technology was understood well enough to illuminate a city, it was not yet widely used across the U.S. economy. Not until the 1920s did electrical power based on the dynamo become sufficiently widespread to be used widely in manufacturing, and to run ordinary electrical appliances like dishwashers and the radio in people's homes.

Before the dynamo, most factories were run on water power, which implied that they had to be physically close to running water and that they had to be laid out so that the machines were aligned with the gears that were turned by the water wheel. Electricity meant that factories could be located in many different places and the machines arranged on different principles. When electricity spread to homes, entire new methods of manufacturing and entire new consumer markets were created. The new computer technology, lest we forget, only became widespread in the 1980s, and the joint revolutions of the Internet and wireless telephone communication only arrived in the 1990s. It may well take several decades for the workplace and the home to gain full access to these technologies and to alter their patterns of use in fundamental ways. Perhaps the productivity boom from computers and telecommunications will actually arrive in 2020, give or take a decade.

Nothing in the official productivity numbers or in the known biases in those numbers suggests that the economy has fundamentally changed its personality in the past few years. However, this conclusion is pessimistic enough, and counterintuitive enough to many knowledgeable observers of the economy, that it must be put forward tentatively. It is inconsistent with a thousand anecdotes from business executives bragging about substantial productivity improvements in their own firms. Often, business leaders can back up their stories with substantial statistical evidence. How can such progress among many individual companies fail to show up when the individual numbers are added up to compute an economy-wide statistic? It may be that the parade of positive anecdotes is not accurate, or that the success stories do not fairly represent the overall business picture, or that official economic statistics are flawed in ways that no one has yet discovered. In the 1980s government statistical agencies experienced substantial budget cuts, and their resources are now disturbingly skimpy. A few million dollars scattered here and there, relative chicken feed in the context of the overall federal budget, could pay for a significant improvement in the accuracy of America's economic data. It would be a small price to pay for a deeper understanding of our $9 trillion economy.

Inflation and the New Economy

The new economy arguments hold that the risk of inflation has declined because of the ways in which globalization and technology put downward pressure on costs. This connection had some truth in the late 1990s. Several of the reasons that inflation stayed low in 1997 and 1998, for example, have to do with foreign trade. Because of the meltdown of economies in East Asia in 1997 and 1998, exports from those countries sold very cheaply on world markets. For the U.S. economy, import prices, not including petroleum, fell about 4 percent per year from 1996–98. Oil prices crashed even faster during these years (although they rebounded somewhat in 1999), partly because weak demand for oil from the struggling East Asian economies helped to produce a glut on the market.

However, these factors are not the only ones that have helped keep inflation low. The high levels of private sector investment in the last few years have meant that the capacity for production in manufacturing and utilities has increased at a rate of nearly 5 percent per year. This has helped to avoid bottlenecks and supply shortages that can lead to inflationary price increases. Another anti-inflation factor is that the rise in medical costs has slowed dramatically. In the late 1980s and early 1990s, inflation in medical costs was typically 6 to 8 percent each year; from 1996 to 1998, thanks largely to the spur of competition and cost control provided by managed care, inflation in medical care costs was only about 3 percent per year. Since health care costs are nearly 14 percent of the U.S. GDP, this change alone had a substantial effect on holding down the overall rise in prices. However, just as past inflation in medical care costs may well have been overstated because the rise in costs included increases in quality as well as a pure rise in prices, it may well be that the reduction in medical care inflation is now partially reflecting a decline in the quality of medical care related to the spread of managed care.

Finally, it should be remembered that inflation looks lower in part because the Bureau of Labor Statistics has adjusted the official measures of inflation for substitution and quality biases. While the reasons for these changes make sense, and the resulting calculations offer a more accurate measure of inflation, the shift in BLS techniques should not fool anyone into thinking that the underlying true inflation rate is actually lower.

Although some factors leading to lower inflation are real enough, it's not clear that they add up to a fundamental shift in the economy toward a permanently low-inflation environment. Low-priced imports and oil and remarkable reductions in computer prices have been holding down inflation, but a disturbance in the Middle East could easily drive oil prices up again, or the eventual recovery of East Asia's economies could end the clearance sale prices for imports, or a weaker American dollar in foreign exchange markets could make imports effectively cost more. Globalization can hold down inflation for a time, but an economy open to global forces can find that these forces sometimes bring inflation, too.

At a more fundamental level, when economists think about inflation in the longer term they steer away from focusing on particular sectors like trade or medical care and focus on the monetary policies of the Federal Reserve. Whatever happens in the rest of the economy, whether these changes ultimately lead to inflation is decided by the response of the Federal Reserve. If the Fed reacts to higher costs—say, an increase in the international price of oil—by expanding the supply of money and credit, inflation will most probably rise. If the Fed does not accommodate such a rise in costs, economic growth will slow, a recession could ensue, and the rate of inflation is likely to fall.

The job of the Federal Reserve in striking the right balance—that is, holding inflation low but not pushing the economy into recession—isn't an easy one. The Fed is trying to juggle priorities of inflation and growth in a world of turbulent economic signals and shifting financial institutions. The relatively limited cost-side pressures in the late 1990s—low prices for imports and oil, limited increases in wages, few capacity bottlenecks—will not last forever. Whether inflation recurs remains fundamentally in the hands of the policy makers at the Federal Reserve and their skill and luck in reacting to the ever-shifting currents of the economy.

Unemployment and the New Economy

Unemployment rates were low during the late 1990s; indeed, they were lower than many economists would have thought possible on a sustainable basis. However, it is not obvious why the "new economy" forces of globalization and new technology should have produced especially low unemployment rates.

Certainly, the ability to export globally may help some firms to create new jobs, but competitive pressure from imports will also cause some firms to lose jobs. Similarly, while jobs are created in a number of new technology industries, those same technologies have allowed waves of downsizing and reductions in middle management at many large corporations. There is no obvious reason to believe that the forces of job creation unleashed by globalization and technology are either larger or smaller than the forces of job destruction that they also create. Most economists believe that while the pressures of global competition and new technology may well reshape employment and wage patterns within and among industries, the overall number of jobs is not altered very much by these factors.

Instead, economists seeking to explain the low rates of unemployment in the last few years often begin by thinking about what level of unemployment constitutes "full employment" for the U.S. economy. In a dynamic economy, where some firms and industries and geographic areas are booming while others are stagnating or declining, some unemployment will arise inevitably as part of the ebb and flow of market forces. The ability of the labor market to adapt flexibly to these changes, and to match willing workers with new employment opportunities, will be influenced by a number of factors: the extent of regulations and taxes imposed on businesses that have the side-effect of increasing the cost of hiring; the structure of welfare and unemployment benefits that can have a side-effect of reducing incentives to work; the power of labor unions and the negotiating strategies they employ; the willingness of workers to move between jobs, industries, and geographic areas; and even the age distribution of the population. As an economy expands out of recession, it creates more jobs until the unemployment rate hits the floor determined by these structural economic factors. One telltale sign that the sustainable level of unemployment has been reached is that further economic expansion tends to produce higher inflation, as labor shortages fuel higher wage costs, rather than cutting unemployment any further.

Thus economists try to estimate the level of sustainable unemployment by looking for that point in the historical data where declines in unemployment level out, and then are followed by rising inflation. In the 1980s and early 1990s, the consensus of main-stream economists was that the rate of sustainable unemployment in the U.S. economy was probably somewhere between 5.5 and 6 percent. This rate of unemployment is sometimes called the NAIRU, an ugly acronym that stands for "non-accelerating inflation rate of unemployment"—that is, how low unemployment can be pushed before inflation begins to accelerate. But for all of 1997 and 1998, the unemployment rate was below 5 percent, without any sign of inflation picking up. What then of beliefs about the NAIRU, which held that unemployment rates this low should cause a labor shortage and a pick-up of inflation? There is no single answer to this question, but several sets of arguments have been proposed.

One set of arguments is that the level of unemployment that the economy could achieve without a risk of inflation decreased between the 1980s and 1990s. Joseph Stiglitz, formerly head of Clinton's Council of Economic Advisers and now chief economist at the World Bank, has argued that three factors have brought down the NAIRU. First, the baby boom generation has reached its prime earning years from ages thirty-five to fifty-four, which means that the U.S. economy now has a relatively large share of middle-aged workers who have a strong attachment to the labor force, and a relatively small share of teenagers, who typically have much higher rates of unemployment. Second, he argues that after decades of low productivity growth, workers have now become accustomed to the idea that their wages may not increase by much from year to year, and so wages that do not rise much do not discourage workers from taking jobs. Finally, the ongoing declines in unionization and the greater competitiveness of the economy as a result of deregulation and, yes, globalization, have made the U.S. labor market more flexible, leading to the possibility of lower sustained unemployment. Taken together, Stiglitz argues, these shifting structural factors might account for the NAIRU falling by 1.5 percentage points; that is, if inflation used to pick up when unemployment went below 5.5 or 6 percent, now inflation would not pick up until unemployment goes below 4 or 4.5 percent.

A second, possibly complementary, set of arguments has to do with the reasons why inflation may have been temporarily constrained in the late 1990s. These reasons were discussed in the previous subsections; they include the low import prices due to weak economies in East Asia and low oil prices worldwide, and also the fact that the measurement of inflation has been changed by the Bureau of Labor Statistics in ways that make the inflation rate appear lower. This argument implies that inflationary pressures are building in the U.S. economy, but they have been held back in the last few years by some one-time causes that seem unlikely to continue forever.

Clearly, estimating the sustainable level of unemployment is far from an exact science. In 1999 the President's Council of Economic Advisers was arguing that the NAIRU was around 5.3 percent, which meant that Clinton's own economists were predicting that the unemployment levels of the last two or three years of the 1990s were unsustainably low in the long term. The Congressional Budget Office is even more pessimistic, basing its longer-term economic forecasts on the prediction that unemployment rates will rise to 5.7 percent by 2003 and then will remain at that level thereafter. However, at least in 1999, the Federal Reserve seemed to have adopted the philosophy that even if the low unemployment rates may presage a rise in inflation at some point, it should wait until it actually sees evidence that inflation is on the rise before it raises interest rates substantially.

The Federal Reserve can enjoy this luxury in large part because in monetary policy, virtue brings its own reward. Inflation is so low in the present partly because the Federal Reserve has been so successful in curbing inflation in the recent past. When people and businesses trust the Federal Reserve and therefore expect little inflation, they are less likely to take actions that lead to higher prices: buyers become more resistant to price increases, sellers are less likely to raise prices, workers are less likely to demand large wage increases, and employers are less likely to agree to substantial wage increases. The expectations of low inflation help generate a reality of low inflation, which creates a virtuous circle of expecting and achieving lower inflation in the future.

In the late 1960s very low inflation could co-exist with very low unemployment, in part because inflation had been so well controlled in the 1950s and the early 1960s. In terms of the relationship between unemployment and inflation, the U.S. economy has now returned to where it was thirty years ago. Today's combination of low inflation and low unemployment may have surprised many economists, but it is not unprecedented. However, when unemployment rates fell below 4 percent in the late 1960s, inflation did finally accelerate. In the late 1990s inflation may have been put to sleep, but if its demise is celebrated too noisily, it could awaken with a start.

Has the New Economy Made Recession Obsolete?

The economic expansion of the 1990s was remarkable for its length. But perhaps even more interesting, this lengthy upswing follows two other long periods without a recession in recent decades: the ninety-two–month upswing from November 1982 to July 1990 and the current reigning champion for length, the 106-month upswing from February 1961 to December 1969. Has something about the new economy made expansions longer and stronger or recessions shorter and weaker?

The impression that economic upswings are growing longer than they were in, say, the late nineteenth century or before World War I has been confirmed by systematic economic studies. The average time from a business cycle trough to a peak has risen from thirty-four months in the period 1886–1916 to fifty-seven months in the period 1948–1999, as shown in Figure 5. However, when economists talk about the reasons for this trend, the new economy forces of globalization and technology do not typically enter the picture. It is sometimes argued that globalization can help bring economic stability, since a nation's firms are no longer totally dependent on domestic demand; for example, domestic firms can continue selling abroad even if the domestic economy slows down, thus blunting the force of recession. This scenario is plausible, but it isn't the only possibility. Events around the world economy— from East Asia to Russia to Brazil—have illustrated an alternative scenario, that global economic tides can bring recession, as well as prosperity.

It is sometimes argued that the forces of computer and telecommunications technology can help with business planning, making it less likely, for example, that businesses will pile up unwanted inventory or make other errors in long-term planning that could destabilize an economy. Again, this is one scenario, and true enough as far as it goes. But the extremely rapid response times allowed by computers and telecommunications eliminate some errors while creating others. The combination of computers, telecommunications, and globalization, for example, are clearly capable of destabilizing national economies as herds of investors stampede in and out of a country's currency and stock markets.

FIGURE 5. Length of Business Cycle Recessions and Expansions:1886 –1999

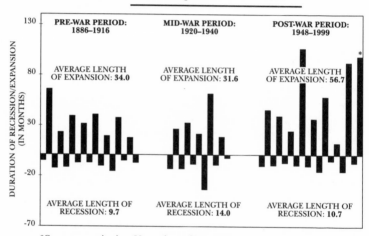

*Current expansion is at 98 months as of May 1999

Source: 1999. Romer, Christina. Journal of Economic Perspectives, pp.30–31.

Setting aside the forces of globalization and technology, plausible reasons why recessions have become farther apart in the United States are not hard to find. One important change is the legal and regulatory infrastructure surrounding banking and finance, everything from deposit insurance to limits on investing on margin to the use of generally accepted accounting principles that make it easier to judge risk. Recessions before World War I were often born in financial panics. Such panics occur less frequently in recent decades, and when they do occur, as in the stock market crash of October 1987, they become short-term blips rather than traumas leading to the collapse of major financial institutions.

A second reason why recessions have become more scarce since World War II is related to fiscal policy. When the economy turns down, welfare and unemployment payments automatically rise. In addition, when the economy turns down, taking income and profit levels with it, the government's tax bite falls automatically. Taken together, these characteristics of transfer payments and the tax system mean that in bad times, lower taxes and higher spending automatically lead to higher budget deficits (or lower surpluses), which help to stimulate the economy. In good economic times, these forces automatically reverse themselves, and growing government budget surpluses (or lower deficits) help prevent the economy from heading into inflationary overdrive. These factors help to explain why it was sensible policy to allow the budget deficit to grow so large in 1991 and 1992—to help the economy recover from recession at that time—and why it was also sensible policy to have budget surpluses in 1998 and 1999—to slow an economy that had been growing strongly.

Finally, the Federal Reserve has become more sensitive to the risks of overreacting, that is, of cutting interest rates so much that inflation results, or of raising interest rates so much that a recession results. In this way, the Fed is reducing the instability that ironically resulted from earlier overexuberant efforts to stabilize the economy.

Conclusions about the Macroeconomy and the New Economy

No one can prove, one way or another, whether the U.S. economy has already experienced a deep structural shift that will lead to the promised land of rapid growth, low unemployment and inflation, and a minimal risk of recession. Only the passage of time will prove or disprove the case. But at the end of the 1990s, the evidence for such a fundamental change rested almost entirely on the facts that the recovery of the 1990s found a second wind around 1996 and continued to be in good health through 1999. There is nothing in the official statistics or in our understanding of the biases in those statistics that suggests that the 1990s have released unprecedented forces that will lead us to a land forever free of such evils as inflation and recession.

When making public policy, it's typically wise to avoid assuming that fundamental changes have occurred, and instead wait for them to be demonstrated.

The mainstream view of the economy in the late 1990s, as enunciated by sources like the Congressional Budget Office and the academics-on-leave who staff Clinton's Council of Economic Advisers, is that the economy has performed better in these last few years than it can be expected to in the long run, thanks to a range of idiosyncratic factors like the fall in oil prices. These experts are not predicting that a recession will occur soon, only that the economy will gradually move back to patterns of growth and unemployment more consistent with historical experience. Early in 1999, for example, the CBO based its predictions for the future on a real GDP growth rate that comes down from nearly 4 percent per year in 1998 to about 2.4 percent a year as a long-term average; on an unemployment rate that rises mildly from the 4.5 percent in 1998 to something more like 5.7 percent as a long-term average; and on a bump in inflation from 1.6 percent in 1998 to perhaps 2.6 percent as a long-term average.

It is quite plausible that the U.S. economy in the late 1990s experienced a fortunate confluence of private sector developments, public policy, and external events that enabled it to perform better than it can over the long run. The claims that globalization and new technology have revolutionized the structure of the U.S. economy, creating a new fast-growing, recession-free economy, are unproven. Yet a shred of doubt remains. Productivity growth was especially strong over the last few years of the 1990s. Many business leaders believe that a substantial economic shift has occurred. It may be that the official statistics have become even more misleading, despite the improvements that have been made, because the quality of what is delivered in today's information and services economy has become ever more difficult to measure.

An Agenda for Productivity Growth

Whether the argument for a "new economy" is a literal truth or the result of over-optimism, the question remains of what economic policies should be followed. We expect that in the years to come, the U.S. economy will continue to suffer occasional spurts of inflation, unemployment, and recession. But with the help of ongoing structural reforms in labor and financial markets, an enlightened policy of automatic transfer and tax stabilizers, and growing knowledge of how to run monetary policy at the Federal Reserve, these swings will continue to be less frequent in the future.

However, the closely linked issues of raising productivity and long-term economic growth remain an ongoing challenge. Productivity growth in the U.S. economy slowed down in the early 1970s, bounced back in the 1980s and early 1990s, and was strong for the last few years of the 1990s. But it is impossible to know whether the resurgence in productivity of the last few years will turn out to be permanent.

This issue is of primary importance in the long run. A higher economic growth rate in each individual year will compound after some years into a substantially larger economy. For example, if the annual growth rate could be just 0.3 percent higher per year for the next thirty years, the GDP would be almost 10 percent larger in the year 2030 than it would otherwise be. An economy that is 10 percent larger will have an easier time dealing with priorities like the costs of Social Security and a graying population, protecting the environment, and dealing with income inequality and poverty—all while still providing a higher standard of living to the average middle class American. The importance of raising the nation's long-term rate of productivity growth, and thus its long-term rate of economic growth, remains just as true even if one believes in the "new economy" arguments. In that case, America is already better off than it realizes. However, it remains true that having an economy that is 10 percent larger in 2030, because of faster growth in the intervening years, would be highly desirable.

The agenda for raising productivity growth stems from thinking about the factors that might raise output per hour in the economy:

greater savings and investment in physical capital; greater investment in human capital (education and job training); improvements in technology; and encouragement of market competition to spur innovation and growth. Let us consider each of these factors in turn.

America's savings rate has long been the lowest among the industrialized nations of the world. A nation's savings rate combines private saving by households, savings by the private sector (which are often directly reinvested by companies), and government saving (which in the case of a government budget deficit becomes negative saving, or borrowing). Year in, year out, the level of national saving in the United States has typically hovered in the range of 15–19 percent of GDP. In many European nations, like France and Germany, national savings is typically more like 22–25 percent of GDP. In Japan, China, and the rapidly industrializing economies of East Asia (at least rapidly industrializing until 1997 and 1998), national savings rates are often in the range of 30 percent of GDP or more.

A nation's savings rate matters, because saving increases wealth for Americans, which enhances the prospects for a higher standard of living in the future. Even in a world where capital flows with increasing ease across national borders, a strong connection remains between a nation's saving rate and its investment rate. Presumably, in a world where capital knew no national borders, this connection would be weakened since there would be no particular reason that a nation that saved a lot would also be the best destination for investing that savings. But the world is still some distance from being a single unified economy; saving does not yet flow immediately and without hindrance from Portland to Paris, or Beijing to Biloxi.

Thus the lower rate of U.S. savings has been reflected in a generally lower rate of U.S. investment. In recent years, U.S. investment as a share of GDP has been higher than its rate of national savings—which means that the U.S. economy is drawing upon foreign savings to make up for the lack of domestic savings. Conversely, countries like Japan and France have had a lower rate of investment than their rate of national savings, because capital from those countries has been flowing abroad.

The U.S. economy has for some years managed to get away with a lower rate of investment in physical capital, thanks to the dynamism of innovation and entrepreneurship in its flexible market economy and to the sophistication of its mature financial sector. But America may not be able to get away with a low savings rate forever. There are at least some models of long-term growth that predict that given present trends, several other nations with higher savings and investment rates will overtake the U.S. level of per capita GDP in the early decades of the twenty-first century.

Creating greater government saving is conceptually straightforward: run larger budget surpluses. Budget surpluses allow paying off the accumulated $3.7 trillion or so of federal debt held by the public, and as investors and banks and mutual funds no longer have their money invested in government bonds, they will be free to invest these funds in the private sector. But although this step is logically straightforward, political support for sustained high surpluses is still uncertain. Many Republicans look at budget surpluses and see a potential tax cut; many Democrats see a potential source of additional spending. In 1999, there was a shaky bipartisan consensus that increasing public saving is a worthwhile use of the budget surpluses, but whether this burst of fiscal prudence will survive future budget battles remains to be seen.

Encouraging private savings by households is not even conceptually straightforward. The problem is that the standard tools— that is, tax incentive savings accounts like Individual Retirement Accounts (IRAs) and 401k accounts—have a perfectly good record of increasing the level of savings in those particular accounts but a less proven record at increasing overall levels of savings. To increase the overall rate of saving, these tools must pass a demanding test; they must increase total private saving by an amount greater than the revenue loss that they cause for the Treasury. There is an enormous controversy within the economics profession as to whether they achieve this goal.

The problem is that people can put funds into these tax-favored savings accounts while drawing down other savings accounts or running up mortgage and credit card debt in such a way that their overall level of savings changes little. Because the amount of tax-favored saving allowed is limited, these tax-favored accounts do not provide any additional incentive to save to anyone who would have saved more than the tax-favored amount in any case. But it might be a mistake to believe that people are extremely rational in their saving behavior. People do odd things, like greatly overwithhold on their income taxes, thus making an interest-free loan to the despised IRS. It may be that tax-favored savings accounts add to saving, not through the marginal incentives that they provide, but rather by attracting attention to the benefits of saving and the miracle of compound interest.

A number of Social Security reform proposals establish mandatory savings plans in an effort to assure that people sock away something for retirement that will replace any cuts in traditional benefits. Such proposals will be discussed in detail in chapter 5, but it can here be noted that like tax-favored savings accounts, mandatory accounts can also be offset by drawing down other assets or by borrowing more.

Another way to push for higher savings is through government policies to increase pension contributions made by companies. Only about 42 percent of current workers are covered by a private pension plan, although a somewhat greater proportion participate in such a plan at some point in their working career. An employee benefit like a pension plan does not come for free, of course. When employers provide pension or health care benefits to employees, over time such benefits tend to come at the cost of lower wages; that is, even if the employer signs the checks, the employee ends up footing the bill indirectly. From this standpoint, proposals for greater private pension coverage are really based on the notion that since employees may not save enough on their own, they should instead be encouraged to save money indirectly, through their employers.

Finally, one might try to encourage savings through an overhaul of the tax system, switching from basing taxation on income earned to basing it on consumption in that year. Savings, and the returns to savings, would only be taxed at the time they are consumed. Some economists have for years advanced arguments for consumption taxes and have even discussed ways that such a tax could be made progressive so that the rich would pay a greater share of their income than the poor. But although a move toward consumption taxes was widely discussed a few years ago, the movement has lost steam. Instead, the agenda for tax policy has turned from pursuing economic goals toward pursuing social goals like assisting families, reducing the marriage penalty, financing education, facilitating the movement from welfare to work, reducing pollution, and numerous other causes.

On the business side, decisions about how much to invest, and how it should be invested, can be affected by the corporate tax code. From the mid-1950s up to 1986, depreciation provisions in the corporate tax code became more generous, allowing business to write off the costs of investment more quickly, and thus to have a tax incentive to invest more. An investment tax credit was periodically provided, often as a way of stimulating the economy in time of recession. These tools to encourage investment were typically used instead of simply lowering the tax on corporate profits, on the grounds that faster depreciation and investment tax credits encouraged new investment while a cut in corporate income tax would only reward past investments. However, many of these provisions were greatly reduced by the Tax Reform Act of 1986, which sought as its general goal to reduce the number of special provisions in the tax code and use the money thus raised to bring down overall tax rates.

There are two arguments against resurrecting the investment tax breaks of old. In the last few years, the level of investment in the U.S. economy has been quite strong, as discussed in chapter 2. For example, investment in producer durable equipment was 6.5 percent of GDP in 1993, but had risen to 8 percent of GDP by 1998. Corporate profits are strong, stock prices are high, and interest rates are low, so companies have relatively easy access to the capital they need. In the longer term, the most powerful argument against adopting targeted investment incentives is that they are difficult to design without favoring—often unintentionally—one form of investment over another. As the allocation of investment becomes determined more by tax laws than by where it is most economically productive, scarce savings are used less and less efficiently. Economic growth and efficiency are usually better served by reducing the amount of targeted incentives so that marginal tax rates can be reduced on all types of saving, investment, and work effort.

Some of the most heated debates related to investment incentives involve proposals for reductions in the capital gains tax. Long-term capital gains, held for more than one year, are now taxed at a maximum rate of 20 percent at the time the gain is actually realized, a tax rate that is well below the top income tax rates, which hover around 40 percent. (The rate is scheduled to fall to 18 percent on assets held over five years.) Because the capital gains tax only applies to gains after they are realized, at the time the asset is sold, it is something of a voluntary tax in that it can be postponed for long periods.

A number of advantages are claimed for a lower capital gains tax rate. It encourages people to buy and sell stocks rather than holding them for a long time out of fear of a higher capital gains tax, which generates more immediate tax revenue for the government. It is supposed to help businesses attract capital. In particular, a capital gains tax cut rewards entrepreneurs who succeed in starting new firms since any gains from stock ownership in the new firm will be worth more.

However, opponents of a capital gains tax cut argue that while lower capital gains taxes do cause more selling and buying of stocks, and thus increase current tax revenues, the lower tax rate also means that capital gains tax revenues are likely to be lower in the middle and long term. Moreover, a substantially lower tax rate for capital gains would stimulate expensive tax avoidance, as tax accountants and lawyers would seek out mechanisms for people to convert ordinary income into capital gains income, and thus take advantage of the lower rate.

But the most important point is that neither the good nor the bad effects of moderate changes in the capital gains tax rate on investment are likely to be very important. Only a portion of the return to business investment takes the form of capital gains, and a relatively small portion of those capital gains is taxed under present law. Capital gains are not taxed at death, and about half of such gains escape taxation as a result. Another one-quarter of business assets resides in tax-deferred forms such as 401k savings accounts. As a result of such provisions, the top statutory capital gains tax rate of 20 percent becomes an effective tax rate of only 7.2 percent, and lowering the statutory rate to, say, 15 percent would only lower the effective tax rate to 6 percent. In a related calculation, the Congressional Budget Office estimates that lowering the top statutory capital gains tax rate from 20 to 15 percent would increase the average after-tax return to saving from only 3 to 3.03 percent. From this perspective, it is difficult to understand why debates over the capital gains tax generate so much heat.

In a modern, knowledge based economy, increasing investment in physical capital is only a starting point to improving productivity. About three-quarters of all output can be traced back to inputs of labor. Some years ago, economists coined the term "human capital" to draw an explicit parallel between investments in machinery and investments in people. While the parallel has offered many useful insights, it is far from perfect. People are more multifaceted than equipment. Investments in human capital aren't just a matter of money going into the education system, but also the time and energy spent by parents with children, and the experience that workers gain on the job. However, it's not altogether clear how public policy can make a substantial difference in helping parents to teach their children. Therefore, much of the policy emphasis has turned to formal education, especially K-12 education.

America has reason for concern with its level of K-12 education. By any quantitative measure, schools did not turn out substantially better students in the 1990s than they did in the 1960s. For example, in 1967 the average verbal score on the Scholastic Assessment Test (SAT) was 543, and the average math score was 516 (both out of 800). By 1997 the average verbal score had declined to 505, and the average math score had more or less held steady at 511. Other standardized tests, like the American College Testing (ACT) program and the National Assessment of Educational Progress, also show a disturbing lack of progress.

There are a variety of arguments over using standardized test scores as a metric for measuring the performance of schools. Maybe today's students have shorter attention spans and more distractions and are harder to educate. Maybe the larger number of single-parent households don't have enough hours in the week to contribute as much to their child's education as they would like. A higher proportion of high school graduates is attending college, so maybe the quality of this group of students has been diluted. Maybe students are learning all sorts of subjects and life skills that no standardized test is measuring. Maybe the difficulty of the tests has changed over time. Maybe, maybe, maybe. But giving reasons for poor performance doesn't make the performance better. Moreover, it's hard to believe that students who do poorly on the sort of basic math that appears on standardized tests are developing unquantifiable math "skills" of the sort that will help them obtain a future career in science or engineering—or even do the sort of basic statistical sampling required in many quality control procedures.

As the U.S. economy moves toward a future that is increasingly based on knowledge and high technology, and where competition with the rest of the world is increasingly fierce, it is crucial to have an education system that is demonstrably providing ever-higher levels of education, rather than just holding its own.

The productivity gains from improving K-12 education are potentially enormous. To give a sense of perspective, John Bishop of Cornell University examined the decline in standardized test scores from 1967 to 1980—a decline equivalent to about 1.25 grade level equivalents. He estimated that the fall-off in SAT scores during that time had made GDP 1 percent lower in 1980 than it would otherwise have been. As this generation of workers then becomes a proportionally larger share of the workers in the economy, the productivity losses continue to mount. Bishop estimated that as a result of the lower test scores from 1967 to 1980, the economy was about 3.6 percent lower by 2000 than it would otherwise have been; in an economy exceeding $8 trillion, that amounts to more than $300 billion that is lost every year. By 2010 the GDP would be 4.4 percent lower.

Bishop's numerical projections involve some background assumptions that can be challenged. However, studies about the returns to education continually raise two broad insights that reach beyond the specific numbers: education is vitally important, and the payoff is far in the future. Imagine that all the schools in the United States were immediately to improve and that over the course of K-12 education the average student would test one full year better in educational accomplishment. This would be an extraordinary improvement in the U.S. education system. But even so, it would be over a decade before the class of graduating high school seniors had experienced the effects of the reform over their entire school career. Given that many of these students will go on to college and graduate school, it will take three or four decades before the students educated at the higher standard dominate the workforce. Thus an improved K-12 education system offers no short-term assistance for America's productivity. An agenda for reforming public education will be discussed in more detail in chapter 4, in the context of assuring equal opportunity to America's children.

When the goal is to increase human capital, there is often somewhat less attention paid to higher education at the college and university level, or to programs to retrain adults. In part, this is because there is a sense that one of the best ways to encourage college enrollments is to have a greater number of well-qualified high school graduates seeking higher education. In part, it is because the high quality of America's system of colleges and universities is the envy of the world already, and there is a sense that the higher education part of America's education system is not what needs fixing. In part, it is because public programs for training (or "retraining") adults to enter the workforce have not been especially successful. It's hard for any relatively short retraining program at the age of twenty-five or thirty-five or forty-five to alter fundamentally the skills and work habits that are already in place at that time. In part, it is because much of the training that happens in the private sector is difficult to describe. It involves the knowledge and problem-solving approaches and attitudes that are absorbed on the job, from coworkers and from the exigencies of situations that arise and only to a far lesser extent from any formal training program offered at the firm. Public policy can be helpful in nurturing on-the-job training by avoiding impediments to hiring unskilled labor, such as overly high minimum wages or other mandated costs associated with hiring. It may go further and provide tax credits for training, but the cost-effectiveness of such credits in stimulating additional training is limited by the fact that much of any credit will be claimed by firms that would have engaged in training in any case. Partly because of the difficulty in designing cost-effective incentives for on-the-job training, reform of the K-12 school system has become the main focus of recent policy discussions.

It is also important to ask whether the nation can do a better job of inducing older workers to stay in the labor force. The strong trend toward earlier and earlier retirement has flattened out in the last few years, but people are still spending longer and longer periods in retirement because of increased life expectancy, even though health and the ability to work have improved. Private pension plans and public policies both provide strong incentives to retire early, and as a result, the economy is losing the services of highly experienced people who possess large amounts of human capital. This issue will be examined in more detail in chapter 5.

Additional physical capital and more highly skilled labor work hand in hand with yet another major source of economic growth: new technology. When economists speak of new technology, they mean not only ostentatiously new inventions like the laser or the semiconductor chip or gene therapy, but also all manner of small innovations that make the same product a little more cheaply, or offer an improved product at a lower cost, or improve the management and organization of the firm making the product. Much of the innovation that occurs in the economy is of this incremental sort; for example, while there have been no extraordinary breakthroughs in the technology behind the laser printer in the last ten years, the cost and the size of machines have fallen dramatically while the quality of output and the speed have increased.

Improvements in technology require a two-part agenda. The first part is encouragement of explicit spending on research and development, which can be thought of as investment in new ideas. The second part is to encourage a competitive market environment, which provides incentives and rewards for those who discover new ways of meeting market demands more successfully—whether those new ways involve scientific breakthroughs or just better management of inventory that has worked so well at Wal-Mart and certain other large retail outlets.

Several basic facts about research and development spending often come as a surprise. First, combined R&D spending by government, private industry, and universities is a relatively small share of the overall U.S. economy, about 2.6 percent of GDP in recent years. Second, R&D spending was about 2.8 percent of GDP in much of the 1960s, dropped off to around 2.2 percent of GDP for much of the 1970s, rebounded back to the area of 2.6 percent of GDP in the 1980s, and has stayed there since. In other words, despite all the talk of how America must embrace technology for its future competitive advantage in the world, the U.S. commitment to R&D spending has essentially kept pace with the economy, no better. Third, if one looks only at civilian oriented nondefense R&D spending, the U.S. spends 2.1 percent of GDP on R&D, which is ahead of much of the rest of the world but lags behind the two other most powerful developed economies in the world—Germany (2.2 percent of GDP on R&D) and Japan (2.7 percent).

Public policy has a variety of tools that might be used to increase R&D spending. The simplest is direct government spending. Of the $220 billion that the U.S. economy spent on R&D in 1998, only about 30 percent, or $66 billion, came from the federal government. Back in the 1960s the federal government funded more than 60 percent of the nation's R&D each year. Now, even though the same share of GDP goes to R&D as it did in the 1960s, the share of R&D funded by the federal government has fallen by half. This decline is almost entirely due to a decline in defense related R&D, which accounted for half of all R&D performed in the U.S. economy in the 1960s, but is now only about 16 percent of all R&D.

It would be helpful for productivity if as the federal government turned away from defense related R&D, a greater share of those resources was funneled toward civilian R&D. Even a relatively small additional commitment of funds in terms of federal spending—say, a raise of $7 billion per year—would raise overall R&D spending (public and private together) by 3 percent per year. After all, there are a number of R&D projects where the potential payoffs are high, but the private sector may not be well motivated to take them on, perhaps because of the uncertainty surrounding the research, or the scale necessary to carry out the research, or the belief that the project may not lead to products that can be profitably marketed in the near future. Despite patent laws, it is often difficult for private innovators to capture much of the economic return to their innovations. Good ideas are too easy to copy, and therefore private markets do not generally provide enough incentive for investments in R&D.

A complementary step is to offer incentives to private industry to carry out additional R&D. The United States enacted a tax credit for research and experimentation in 1981 and has been tinkering with it, and occasionally allowing it to expire before renewing it, ever since. A number of studies have found that the tax credit is an effective way of stimulating private R&D spending; for example, one study found that a $1 reduction in the price of R&D as a result of the tax credit stimulates approximately $1 of additional R&D in the short run, and an additional $2 of R&D in the long run. Whatever the current effectiveness of the R&D credit, it is generally agreed that it would be even more effective if it were made permanent rather than renewed one year at a time, so that firms could rely on it for long-term planning.

The fundamental determinants of productivity growth are the interaction of physical capital, human capital, and new technology. However, these factors need to come together in a competitive market environment, where there are pressures and rewards for being innovative and efficient. The U.S. economy has taken several important steps in this direction in recent decades. The increase in globalization discussed at several points in this chapter involves a substantial increase in the competitive opportunities and pressures faced by many U.S. firms. Starting in the late 1970s, the U.S. also carried out a grand experiment with deregulation of many industries, including airlines, trucking, railroads, banking, long-distance phone service, and oil. The results of that increase in competition are widely accepted to have been good for consumers to the tune of perhaps $60 billion in lower prices every year, and good for incentives to innovate as well. Because of the success of past deregulation efforts, the U.S. appears likely to push for greater deregulation in local phone service and in electricity generation in the next few years.

But the delicate balancing act of drawing lines between socially useful market competition and socially unproductive blocking of competition is never quite complete. The U.S. economy saw wave upon wave of corporate mergers and acquisitions throughout the 1990s. Some doubtless contribute to firms being more productive, slimmed-down, tougher competitors; others act only to entrench incumbent firms against competition, while doing little for consumers or innovation. It is the task of the antitrust authorities at the Department of Justice and the Federal Trade Commission to tell the difference.

Perhaps the toughest and certainly the most talked about antitrust case in the last few years involves Microsoft, which has been accused by the U.S. government of wielding its powerful position in the software market to discourage competitors unfairly. Wisely, the government case did not seek to argue that consumers have already been damaged by Microsoft; given the soaring capabilities and plunging prices of computer software, that case would have been difficult to make. Moreover, the government did not seek to argue that the simple fact of Microsoft's dominant share of the software used for running personal computers was illegal in and of itself. For quite a few years now, *being* a monopoly has not been illegal, but if a firm is a monopoly, then it is subject to a heightened level of scrutiny, and certain actions it takes may be illegal. Driving competitors out of business is not illegal, in and of itself, either. So the government case against Microsoft is a delicate one, based on arguing that by taking certain actions, like making it hard for the software of competitors to be added to the Microsoft system or by making it hard to delete certain parts of Microsoft software, the firm was exploiting its monopoly position unfairly. Whatever the eventual outcome of the specific Microsoft case, it helps to illustrate that even in the world of rapid change and high technology, there will be issues of how best to preserve an active competitive environment that will spur additional innovation.

Two sorts of policies that are often mentioned for stimulating economy have not been emphasized here, but deserve mention, if only in a negative sense. One set of policies involves public spending on infrastructure; the other involves "expansionary" macroeconomic policy.

Public infrastructure projects are often supported at least in part because of a sense that they help productivity growth. Certainly, the economy works better with roads and bridges and airports and telephone lines than it would work without those elements, and one recommendation often made to low-income countries of the world as they seek to develop is that they need to build up a transportation and communications infrastructure.

However, in a democracy, infrastructure investments often become a type of currency used to cement political deals. Politicians love highways; after all, they are highly visible and they employ people in the district. Studies by the Congressional Budget Office indicate that infrastructure investments—often referred to as "pork barrel spending"—do not tend to go where rates of return as determined by cost-benefit studies are highest.

Differentiating worthy infrastructure projects from political boondoggles can only be done on a case-by-case basis. But many economists would agree with two generalizations about such projects. First, when building such projects, it is important to invest for the long term. For example, economists have made estimates that if the standard thickness of pavement was increased from 11.2 inches to 13.8 inches, the life of the pavement before serious repairs are needed would more than double. Second, trying to build enough infrastructure so that there will never be congestion is a mug's game. It makes no sense to expand continually highways or airports or phone lines that will be used to capacity only, say, for fifteen minutes on each weekday, and thus be used at less than capacity for the other 166 hours and 45 minutes of each week. Instead, it makes sense to offer incentives for people to spread out their peak-load use over broader periods of time. Economists often advocate using tolls or charges on peak-load users to accomplish this purpose. Surely, there are some cases in the United States where roads need to be built or airports expanded. But there are many, many more cases where imposing charges to spread out peak-load usage would both raise money to fund any necessary expansions of infrastructure and also reduce the need for expanding that infrastructure in the first place.

Expansionary macroeconomic policy includes several policy tools: tax cuts, spending increases, and lower interest rates. These are the same policies that can be used to fight a cyclical downturn in the economy. The reason they are not mentioned in the context of productivity growth is that while these policies are capable of giving the economy a good swift kick to help lift it out of recession, there is little reason to believe that they have much impact in creating a sustained increase in productivity over time. Instead, these macroeconomic tools simply increase the level of buying power and demand in the economy. Pouring demand into the economy can help an economy perform at capacity—but productivity growth is a matter of expanding that capacity over time through investments in physical capital, human capital, and technology. If an aggressive attempt were made to stimulate the economy with more demand, at a time when the economy is already close to capacity (or even temporarily a little beyond full capacity), the result will not be greater productivity growth, but merely a surge of inflation. The only way to build a sustained increase in productivity growth is through the intertwined combination of investment in physical and human capital, occurring in a context of market incentives that encourage innovation and efficiency.

How Much Can Policy Boost Economic Growth?

If the "new economy" argument is true, then the U.S. economy may already have boosted its growth rate. This conclusion is a cheerful one, until you contemplate the reality that the United States is certainly not the only economy in the world being influenced by forces of globalization and new technology. At best, the U.S. economy might claim that today it is benefiting to a greater extent from these forces—but there is no particular reason that advantage should continue to hold true. If the U.S. wants to continue to lead the nations of the world in standard of living, as well as to provide resources for addressing the issues of tomorrow, it is vital to start thinking now, right away, this year, about a comprehensive agenda to raise the rate of productivity growth.

If the United States were to make a concerted policy effort along many of the dimensions discussed here to boost long-term economic growth, what might it achieve? One sometimes hears wild boasts from politicians on the campaign trail that this policy or that one might boost U.S. productivity levels to 4 percent per year, 5 percent per year, or even more. One often hears parallels to nations that achieved annual rates of GDP growth approaching 10 percent per year or more, like Japan in the 1960s or China in the 1980s. Why can't the United States dramatically raise its rate of economic growth like these other nations?

The main reason, of course, is that those nations were much poorer to begin with; for example, China was among the poorest nations in the world before its growth spurt of the last few decades. Less developed economies typically have greater opportunities for rapid growth; in particular, they can initially grow rapidly by borrowing institutional lessons and technological advances from more developed nations. But as a nation becomes wealthier, it becomes harder to maintain those hyperbolic rates of economic growth, as Japan has discovered in recent years.

There are no precise estimates of the possible rates of economic growth available to the United States if a large number of productivity enhancing policies were enacted. Optimists point to the years after World War II, when the U.S. economy was expanding into the rest of the world, when education was rising quickly thanks to the GI Bill, and when the economy could take advantage of a variety of new technologies originally developed during wartime. This scenario might imply raising the labor productivity growth rate from about 1.6 percent per year in the 1990s back to the post–World War II levels of perhaps 3 percent per year. Those less optimistic might point out that the size of the U.S. economy has tripled (after adjusting for inflation) since the 1960s, which implies that many of the opportunities for growth available in earlier times have already been exploited. Consequently, it may be harder to sustain a rate of growth as rapid as existed in those years after World War II, and before the growth slowdown of the early 1970s. Even with a highly favorable policy agenda, perhaps the average rate of productivity growth would only rise from 2 percent per year to, say, 2.5 percent per year.

Such modest prospects for higher productivity growth may seem disturbing. Is all of this discussion just much ado about almost nothing—that is, a few tenths of a percent? Yes and no; yes, the argument is indeed over changing growth rates by 1 percent per year or even less, and no, this difference is far from negligible. Remember that the rate of productivity growth is an annual rate over a sustained period of time, so that the additional growth accumulates each year. The U.S. GDP in 1998 was roughly $8 trillion. If it grows at a real rate of 2 percent per year (ignoring inflation), it would reach $15.1 trillion by 2030. If it grew at 2.5 percent per year, because of 0.5 percent per year faster productivity, it would reach $17.6 trillion by 2030. Notice that even with only half a percent of extra growth per year, after three decades the economy is more than $2 trillion larger—or larger by roughly one-sixth. Figure 6 illustrates the different paths of the GDP between 1999 and 2030 under the assumptions of 1 percent, 2 percent, and 3 percent growth.

FIGURE 6. Real Gross Domestic Product (GDP): 1960–2030

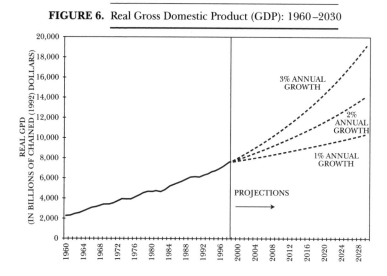

Source: Author's calculations and 1999. The Economic Report of the President. Table B-2.

Moreover, remember that these accumulated multitrillion dollar gains from productivity are not one-time gains, but continue in perpetuity. In the long run, nothing is more important for the overall health and welfare of the economy than to develop and sustain a positive environment for economic growth.

4

Inequality and Opportunity: Winners and Losers in the New Economy

The argument that free market capitalism benefits society is rooted in the incentives capitalism provides for innovation and hard work, the flexibility it offers in response to changing conditions, and the resulting patterns of efficiency and growth. But in the midst of this charge toward economic growth and efficiency are people. Some will be lifted up by the market economy; others will be cast down.

The different outcomes experienced by individuals are partly a matter of individual choice; those who work hard, save their money, and update their skills and knowledge will tend to have a higher standard of living than those who do not. But intertwined with these personal decisions is an inextricable component of inherited circumstances and raw luck. The person who is born into a family with two involved and well-educated parents and a middle class or better level of income is more likely to succeed in the modern economy than someone who is born into less fortunate circumstances. There are exceptions to this general rule, of course, but the fact that some people manage to overcome obstacles does not mean that the obstacles did not exist in the first place.

Luck also plays a role. People differ in their natural abilities, ranging from physical capabilities to intelligence. Some people go to work for a struggling company that turns into Microsoft; other people go to work for a struggling company that goes bankrupt. Some workers are at firms whose top managers make smart decisions; some workers of equal talent, through no fault of their own, are at firms where the managers drive the firm into the ground. Some people are in industries where new competitors arrive, either from new domestic sources or from abroad; others can be secure in their jobs without facing such a challenge.

Thus the market oriented American economy is a mixed blessing: it provides incentives for efficiency and growth, but it causes risk and insecurity in the process. Even when people recognize that competition and free trade are good for the economy as a whole, they can also support government efforts to reduce the level of risk faced by those whom the market leaves behind. There is no contradiction in supporting both a free market and a government safety net; indeed, one can believe that the safety net makes it easier for society as a whole to live with the turmoil and risk of free markets. The challenge is to design a safety net that provides adequate protections without crippling people's incentives to improve their own lives in the process.

After reviewing some basic facts about poverty, inequality, and job insecurity, this chapter considers what might be done to shore up incomes at the bottom and to increase opportunity. We emphasize, in particular, the importance of "making work pay" for low-skilled adults and of interventions early in life that can help people move up the economic ladder in the future. Little public support exists, in our view, for government assistance that is not tied to work among able-bodied adults. However, there is strong public support for policies to assist the large number of children whose schools and family environments all too often condemn them to the bottom rungs of society. The 1996 welfare reform law fundamentally changed the character of America's safety net. It is time to strengthen and rebuild the ties of American public policy to the poor, not by reshuffling incomes or reinventing welfare yet again, but by subsidizing work, promoting strong families, and insisting on high-performance schools.

The Rise in Inequality and Poverty

There is no serious disagreement among experts in the field that inequality of incomes has increased in the United States over the last few decades. One straightforward method of measuring inequality is to look at how much income the best off families have in comparison to the worst off. Figure 7 does this by tracking the ratio of mean incomes in the top fifth of the population to mean incomes in the bottom fifth and showing that this ratio has grown since 1970.

FIGURE 7. Ratio of Mean Income of the Highest Fifth to Income of the Lowest Fifth

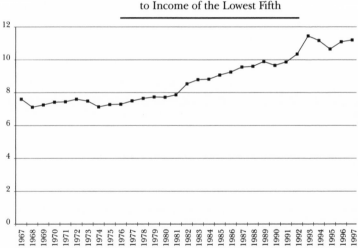

Source: 1997. Center on Budget and Policy Priorities, Poverty and Income Trends, p. 59.

Another way to look at the issue is to compute the share of income received by different segments of the population. In 1974 the poorest fifth of the population received 5.7 percent of the total income in that year, whereas the richest fifth received 40.6 percent; by

1997 the bottom fifth (those with incomes below $15,400 in that year) received 4.2 percent of the income while the share received by the top quintile (those with incomes above $71,500) had risen to 47.2 percent. The income distribution was fairly stable from 1950 until the late 1960s or early 1970s. Then the share of income going to the top fifth of the income distribution, and particularly to the top 5 percent, began to grow. The rise for the top quintile, an increase of 6.6 percentage points of the income pie, was almost all accounted for by the 5.9 percentage point increase going to the top 5 percent of the income distribution. These changes are illustrated in Table 1. The rise in inequality topped out about 1993; since then, inequality has more or less remained at its new, higher level.

TABLE 1 Share of Aggregate Income Received by Each Fifth and Top 5 Percent of Families: 1950 to 1997

| Year | Shares of aggregate income | | | | | Top 5 percent |
	Lowest fifth	Second fifth	Third fifth	Fourth fifth	Highest fifth	
1997	4.2	9.9	15.7	23.0	47.2	20.7
1995	4.4	10.1	15.8	23.2	46.5	20.0
1990	4.6	10.8	16.6	23.8	44.3	17.4
1985	4.8	11.0	16.9	24.3	43.1	16.1
1980	5.3	11.6	17.6	24.4	41.1	14.6
1975	5.6	11.9	17.7	24.2	40.7	14.9
1970	5.4	12.2	17.6	23.8	40.9	15.6
1965	5.2	12.2	17.8	23.9	40.9	15.5
1960	4.8	12.2	17.8	24.0	41.3	15.9
1955	4.8	12.3	17.8	23.7	41.3	16.4
1950	4.5	12.0	17.4	23.4	42.7	17.3

Source: U.S. Bureau of the Census, Current Population Survey.

The mere existence of inequality of incomes is not especially troubling. No one would expect the income distribution to be completely equal, that is, that each fifth of the income distribution would receive exactly 20 percent of total income. After all, it is reasonable to expect that people in mid-career will have higher earnings than those just starting out, or than those in retirement. In any given year, some people may suffer a temporary loss of income, perhaps due to unemployment, while others experience a temporary gain, perhaps by working overtime. Graduate students who are poor one year may be very well off five years later, while a house-wife whose husband leaves her may suffer a sharp drop in income. But fluctuations in income for these or other reasons will tend to even out over time.

Indeed, one sometimes hears it argued that the growth in wage inequality since the mid-1970s doesn't much matter, because the inequality figures don't take this kind of income mobility into account. In the end, this argument doesn't hold much water. It is true that measures of inequality expressed at any given time do not reveal the extent to which people are moving up and down the income ladder. The empirical evidence on mobility shows that between 25 and 40 percent of adults move between quintiles of the income distribution in any given year; and about 60 percent change quintiles over a nine-year period. The evidence also shows that the degree of mobility in the income distribution hasn't changed in recent decades. Thus the observed rise in income inequality has not been offset by a greater degree of mobility. Moreover, international studies offer the discomforting evidence that U.S. mobility between income quintiles is no better than in many European countries, although those economies have more equal income distributions.

Many people find the evidence about rising inequality less troubling than a related trend: the evidence of a rise in poverty. It can reasonably be argued that there is nothing wrong with more people earning high incomes, as long as there are also fewer individuals mired in poverty with insufficient resources to provide for themselves and their families. The poverty rate—that is, the proportion of all individuals living in families below government defined poverty lines for different sized families—tends to rise in recessions and fall during economic upswings. However, the general level of poverty has gradually increased over the past two decades and stood at 13.3 percent in 1997, as shown in Figure 8. Among the elderly, the poverty rate was 10.5 percent. Among children under eighteen, the poverty rate was 19.2 percent; rates among black and Hispanic children were roughly twice as high.

The level of the poverty line has been a subject of some controversy. The poverty line was originally set back in the mid-1960s, and since then it has been adjusted for inflation from year to year.

FIGURE 8. Poverty Rate: 1973–1997

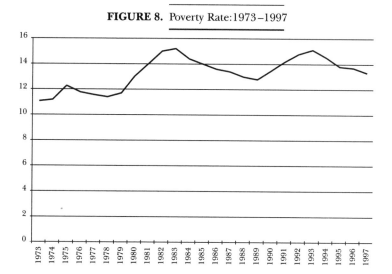

One concern is that the poverty rate is based on pre-tax income, which may understate the degree of deprivation because income is measured before taxes, and poor families who work are subject to payroll taxes and sometimes to income taxes. Conversely, however, the tax liabilities of poor families have been more than offset by the availability of the Earned Income Tax Credit. The EITC is refundable; that is, any portion of the credit not needed to offset tax liabilities is provided as a direct subsidy to low-income families at the end of the year. As a result, many working poor families actually have more after-tax credit income than is recognized in the official data. In addition, since the poverty rate is based on income, it does not include the value of noncash benefits provided by Medicare, Medicaid, food stamps, or subsidized housing. Moreover, a poverty rate based on income does not capture the fact that poor families in the 1990s often own items that would have been luxuries or did not yet exist a few decades ago, like color televisions and portable phones. Because of economic growth and the creation of new products, the middle class of the 1950s would marvel at many of the products readily available to poor households in the 1990s. Finally, poor families, on average, consume more each year than their measured incomes, suggesting that either they have unreported income and assets, or some ability to borrow, or that they are poor only temporarily.

The bottom line is that poverty can be measured in a variety of ways: the official poverty rate based on pre-tax income, or income after taxes and cash transfers, or income adjusted for in-kind transfers, or consumption. However, the typical pattern that arises from looking at a variety of such measures is that while average poverty rates do fluctuate with the business cycle, and the meaning of poverty evolves over time as the economy grows and changes, poverty has been creeping higher over the last two decades.

Since the poverty line is a fixed income level (according to size of household) adjusted upward for inflation, one might expect that over time, growth of the economy would cause fewer and fewer people to end up below the poverty line. In a relative sense, the poor are always with us, but with an absolute poverty line adjusted only for inflation, poverty rates should decline as a society becomes more affluent. Thus the fact that the amount of poverty has increased over recent decades as the economy has grown is somewhat surprising. One possibility is that this is a statistical illusion caused by a failure to measure inflation properly. If the poverty line increases according to the measured rate of inflation each year, but the measured inflation rate overstates the true inflation rate (for the reasons discussed in chapter 3), then the poverty line will be raised higher than true inflation would justify, making the poverty rate appear higher. Another possibility is that the economy has indeed grown but that few of the benefits have trickled down to the poor. This latter interpretation is consistent with the rise in income inequality that has occurred.

What Are the Causes of the Growth in Inequality and Poverty?

Measures of inequality and poverty need not always move together. A change in the top tax rate, for example, affects the distribution of income, but not the rate of poverty. Conversely, a reduction in the cost-of-living adjustment in Social Security will move a number of near-poor elderly from just above the poverty line to just beneath it, thus affecting the poverty rate but having only a tiny effect on measures of overall inequality. But with these concerns noted, the movements in income inequality and poverty are similar enough to consider them together. The rise in inequality and poverty is usually attributed to three factors: changes in family composition, changes in the economy, and changes in public policy.

Changes in the living arrangements of individuals account for much of the rise in both poverty and inequality. An increasing proportion of households is headed by a single adult, usually a woman with limited earning power. In addition, more married households now have two paychecks, and high earners are increasingly marrying one another. Unlike the old days of the strongly gender-segregated workplace, when a male doctor might marry a female nurse, or a male professor might marry a secretary, now doctors and professors are marrying each other. These demographic trends can explain between one-half and two-thirds of changes in both poverty and inequality over the last few decades.

Another important reason for rising poverty and inequality is changes in the economy that have produced greater wage inequality. In particular, wages have increased among better educated or more-skilled workers relative to those with less skill. In 1963 a college graduate earned about 45 percent more than a high school graduate. By the late 1960s the differential had risen to 60 percent, but it then fell back to about 45 percent by the late 1970s. However, the differential then began to climb, and by the early 1990s a typical college graduate was earning 80 percent more than a typical high school graduate. Real wages for male workers with only a high school degree have actually declined over the last few decades, making it increasingly difficult for them to support a family.

The reasons for rising wage inequality are something of a mystery. For one thing, one can find greater inequality almost everywhere one looks—for example, within occupations and industries, and even among workers with the same amount of education. While the average college graduate is earning more than the average high school graduate, the earnings of high school graduates and college graduates, considered separately, have also become much more unequal, which indicates that while the average returns to education have risen, these returns have also become more variable and uncertain.

There is no proven single factor that has caused this rise in the inequality of wages, no smoking gun, only a lot of plausible stories that are hard to confirm with solid evidence. The stories often begin with the keystones of the "new economy" discussed in chapter 3, that is, the spread of globalization and of new technology. As more production processes are automated, businesses need workers who can program and repair machines, not just operate them. In offices, they need skilled support staff to use the now ubiquitous desktop computers, not legions of less-skilled secretaries and clerks without such skills. Those at the bottom of the income distribution, who have less access to this technology and less training in how to use it, have lost out. Moreover, thanks to globalization, these low-skilled workers face heightened competition from workers in low-wage countries abroad, who may be earning a fraction of the U.S. minimum wage, thereby putting downward pressure on the earnings of less-skilled U.S. workers.

As between these two explanations, most economists believe that technology has been more important than trade. Imports are still only about 13 percent of the U.S. GDP, and imports from low-wage countries—like Mexico and Indonesia—are half or less of that total. True, imports from poor countries have increased some in recent decades, but it is unlikely that imports representing this relatively small share of the economy could be responsible for the dramatic shift in wage patterns that has been observed. Moreover, many low-wage workers in the United States are in service industries—say, giving haircuts, cleaning homes, answering telephones, delivering packages—and these sorts of jobs probably compete less directly with low-wage workers abroad. It's hard to hire someone living in Botswana to deliver a pizza. So it is not obvious why globalization should powerfully affect wages in many domestic service industries, one way or the other. For these and other reasons, most economists believe that only a modest proportion of growing wage inequality can be attributed to trade.

The direct evidence in favor of the technology explanation is limited. Workers who use computers at work appear to earn 10–15 percent more than those who do not, and a rising proportion of all workers uses a computer on the job (about half, up from a quarter in the early 1980s). But the primary reason for thinking technology may be important is because most other explanations have been found wanting. In addition, the technology explanation is consistent with the fact that wages for better educated workers have shot up at the same time that more and more people were completing high school and moving on to college. When the supply of something goes up, the typical reaction of economists is to expect its price to go down. If instead the price is rising, if college educated workers are earning ever-higher wages relative to those with only a high school education, the pattern strongly suggests that the demand for college educated workers, or skilled labor more generally, from businesses was rising even faster than the supply, thus driving up its relative wage.

Eventually people are likely to respond to this situation by acquiring still more education, which should cause the premium for skills to stop rising, and then to shrink. Some recent data suggest that this process may have begun to occur in the second half of the 1990s.

Globalization and technology are not the only potential culprits for greater wage inequality. At least three other changes have occurred over the last two decades that might be expected to injure the earnings of low-wage workers. The first is a decline in the minimum wage. Because the value of the minimum wage was not adjusted upward between 1981 and 1989, its real value was eaten away by inflation, and it declined by one-third from 1978 to 1989. However, increases in the minimum wage since 1996 have increased its value by about 20 percent, so that it is now only about 15 percent less than it was in the late 1970s. A second is declining union membership. Unions tend to create more equal wages among their workers, and in particular to raise the wages of those toward the bottom of the income distribution. But the share of wage and salary workers in the U.S. belonging to a union fell from 26 percent in 1974 to 14 percent in 1997. The third factor is rising immigration into the United States. Immigration has been high in recent decades, and immigrants are increasingly low skilled.

Economists disagree on how much weight to give to each of these factors. But mainstream opinion holds that the single most important cause of the rise in wage inequality is a technology induced increase in the demand for more skilled workers, with the other factors best thought of as contributing to some lesser extent.

Public policy, in the form of taxes and benefit programs, can off-set or exacerbate these changes in the economy. Back in the 1980s, some politicians and advocates attributed the rise in inequality to President Reagan's economic policies, including tax cuts for the rich and slashing welfare for the poor. However, Republican tax and welfare policies of the 1980s cannot be the primary culprit for at least three reasons.

First, the rise in inequality was substantially due to greater in-equality in pre-tax income, not incomes measured after taxes and the receipt of government benefits. Second, a rise in inequality was also observed in a number of other economies, although not to the same extent that it was seen in the United States, which seemed to rule out explanations that were heavily rooted in U.S. tax or welfare policies. Finally, the rise in inequality started well before Reagan as-sumed office, and continued at least to the early Clinton years. That said, changes in tax and benefit programs during the decade of the 1980s did nothing to compensate for the growing gap be-tween rich and poor and, according to some studies, did contribute modestly to that gap.

None of this should imply that changes in public policy cannot have important effects on the level of inequality. In fact, the pro-gressive tax code, in which the rich pay a higher proportion of their income in taxes than the poor, has been estimated to reduce one measure of inequality by 6 percent, and cash and noncash benefits have been estimated to reduce inequality by 18 percent (as mea-sured by what economists call a Gini coefficient). Furthermore, if it is assumed, somewhat improbably, that taxes and transfers do not affect work or saving behavior, then about 30 million people, or half of those who would have been poor in the absence of such taxes and benefits, are removed from poverty by the existence of currently available assistance. Even if the behavioral response to such assistance is considered, it is likely that a very large proportion of the 30 million removed from poverty by assistance would not have been able to escape poverty by an increased effort to work or save.

How Real Are Concerns
about Job Insecurity?

There is widespread popular concern that jobs have become more insecure, that layoffs have become more widespread, that the chance of staying with an employer for a lifetime is falling. These arguments were heard with particular vehemence during and immediately after the recession of 1990–91. But the hard evidence offers only mixed support for this view.

The government has since 1984 carried out a Displaced Worker Survey, which looks at workers who have lost their jobs involuntarily because of a plant closing, abolition of their job, or a layoff. The 1998 survey revealed that about 12 percent of workers had been displaced in the previous three years; this displacement rate was higher than in the 1990 survey, carried out before the recession of 1990–91, but lower than in the 1992, 1994, and 1996 surveys. The 1998 survey also found that only 24 percent of displaced workers were not employed at another job within one to three years, which was lower than in any of the previous surveys since the first one in 1984, which found that 30–42 percent of displaced workers had not found another job within one to three years after losing their job.

Another measure of job security looks at the number of people who are in jobs that they have held for a long period of time. For example, in 1979 about 40 percent of all workers were in a job that they had held for ten years or more; in 1996 35 percent of all workers were in a job they had held for ten years or more. The decline in job tenure among men has been larger than this, but is masked in the overall data by increasing job tenure among women as a result of their growing commitment to the workforce.

The statistics on job security can be sliced and diced in many ways, and certainly not all the news is good. For example, analysis of the reasons for job loss in the early 1990s suggests that a higher proportion of such losses at that time was due to permanent as opposed to temporary layoffs, compared with earlier time periods with comparable unemployment rates. Moreover, although most of those who lose jobs find new ones, they typically suffer a loss of earnings in the process. Of those displaced from their jobs in 1991–92, only about a third subsequently found full-time work at the same or higher pay.

Overall, taking the good with the bad, the picture of job insecurity that is painted by the data is not as bad as many people—or at least many journalists—seem to believe. It's interesting to speculate on why there is such a strong belief that jobs have become much more insecure when the evidence on the point is rather thin. One possible reason is because job insecurity is no longer just a blue collar concern; an increasing number of more visible and more vocal white collar workers, including middle managers, have been affected by corporate restructurings and downsizing. A second reason is that many people seem to overestimate how many workers stayed with an employer for the long term in the past. The U.S. labor market has long been a fluid place in which most workers hold a number of jobs before the age of thirty and then switch again a few more times in the rest of their working life. So in the 1990s perhaps less changed than meets the eye.

Even if job security has not changed a great deal, there is still a role for government to play in easing the blow for those who lose jobs unexpectedly and involuntarily. Unemployment insurance, in which employed workers pay into the program and newly unemployed workers receive benefits for a limited time while between jobs, is perhaps the best example of such a program. However, the unemployment insurance system was built on the premise that layoffs were temporary and that there would be a job to go back to. This pattern may be less applicable today than in the past, and it may make more sense to help workers retrain for new positions, to examine policies that would lead to greater portability of health and pension benefits, and to establish more effective forms of labor market information and job search assistance. Although training programs for dislocated workers have had, at best, a mixed record of success, evidence from several studies both in the United States and Europe suggests that government programs that focus on helping people learn how to locate and apply for jobs can be cost-effective.

The case for all these programs is not that jobs have become much more insecure in the 1990s; it is that in a capitalist economy, jobs have always been somewhat insecure and are still insecure. If American society is to embrace the machinery of capitalism, it should also assure that the machine is oiled to help it run more smoothly.

Ending Welfare as We Knew It

In 1996 Congress and President Clinton took a bold step in the face of evidence that poverty and inequality had been rising for several decades. America's welfare system was overhauled by the Personal Responsibility and Work Opportunity Reconciliation Act, which was the fulfillment of President Clinton's campaign pledge to "end welfare as we know it." The previous welfare program, Aid to Families with Dependent Children (AFDC), was replaced by the Temporary Assistance for Needy Families (TANF) program.

The new name heralded a number of changes. First, the length of benefits received under TANF is limited: no one can receive federally funded benefits for more than five years during a lifetime. Second, TANF converts the $16 billion or so in federal funding for AFDC into a block grant to the states, giving each state much greater freedom to decide how to spend the money. Third, participants are required to work at the end of two years, and states must put an increasing proportion of their initial caseloads in a "work activity," with the percentage rising 5 percent per year until it reaches 50 percent in 2002. A "work activity" could include a job in the private or public sector, on-the-job training, or even a limited period of job search and job readiness assistance.

Under the AFDC system, welfare benefits were an entitlement; if you met the rules for eligibility, you were entitled to receive the legally set level of benefits in your state (which varied widely from $120 a month in Mississippi in 1997 to $639 in Vermont for a family of three with no other earnings). Nothing in the new rules requires that families retain eligibility for any particular level of welfare benefits. Under AFDC, states were required to match federal spending on welfare, and under TANF, they are required to maintain their previous effort by spending at least 75 percent of what they spent under AFDC. However, if a state spends the necessary minimum amount and meets the work requirements, it can set shorter time limits, lower benefit amounts, or boot people off the welfare rolls entirely for failure to comply with various requirements. A state can also invest in child care or job training, subsidize earnings, and do a host of other things with the TANF funds as long as they are targeted on needy families with children.

Clearly, this new system offers a lot of flexibility and encourages states to experiment with new approaches to reducing poverty and welfare dependence. The overall intention of the program is to make welfare time-limited and to push poor people back into the workforce vigorously. The law assumes that the poor are best served by encouraging them to become self-supporting rather than by handing out money indefinitely. To what extent has the program succeeded?

During the first two years since the welfare reform act, from 1996 to 1998, welfare caseloads declined by about a third. There have been many stories of families moving from welfare to work, and relatively few stories of families where the change has imposed substantial hardship. According to a variety of studies, about two-thirds of all those who leave welfare find jobs although their earnings are very modest—typically, $6 to $8 an hour. Very little is known about the other one-third. Some may be living with boyfriends or other family members; some may have unreported earnings; and some may be facing real hardship.

Despite this heartening beginning, a number of worries lurk just under the surface. Now that the most work-ready welfare recipients have been pushed into the labor market, many of the remaining welfare recipients have personal problems, such as impaired mental health, an abusive relationship, or a substance abuse problem. Growth in the economy has been strong in the few years since the passage of the welfare reform act in 1996, so it has been relatively easy for the most job-ready of those receiving welfare to join the work force. Sooner or later, unemployment rates will rise, which will make it harder for low-skilled individuals to find jobs. In addition, welfare caseloads typically rise dramatically during recessions, but since the federal block grant is no longer linked to the size of the caseload, states may be forced to reduce or terminate benefits under the resulting fiscal pressures. Although some "rainy day" funds exist in case a recession occurs, and Congress could always vote additional money if the need arises, it remains unclear how the extra welfare costs associated with a recession will be paid.

The primary goal of the welfare reform act of 1996 is worthy, that is, helping welfare recipients to support themselves. However, the success of the act in its first few years may be deceptive; in part, it is a matter of skimming the cream by getting the most work-ready welfare recipients back on the job in a very favorable economic environment. Dealing with those welfare recipients who are not worth the minimum wage to any employer in a slack economy will be a different challenge altogether, and may well require either substantial reforms to the 1996 act or more creativity by the states. All in all, however, the new law has been much more successful to date than many experts would have predicted.

A Policy Agenda for the Working Poor

When it comes to designing public policy, it isn't always essential to know why levels of inequality or poverty have increased. If you have a cold, it doesn't always matter how you got it; aspirin, fluids, and rest are still the cure. Many of the causes of rising inequality may be difficult to reverse, or even undesirable to reverse, like the spreading use of computer technology. But that doesn't mean that the symptoms cannot be addressed.

In the past, the primary response to poverty was welfare and related noncash benefits such as food stamps, Medicaid, and housing assistance. However, as more women at every income level have entered the labor force, the social consensus has shifted in favor of expecting able-bodied adults to work, including the mothers of young children. At the same time, in a little-noticed series of legislated changes in existing programs such as Medicaid and the EITC, federal support for the working poor has increased considerably since the early 1980s. In this section, we address what might be done to further help the so-called working poor, meaning those who remain poor or near poor, even if at least one parent works full time.

For a low-skilled worker, supporting a family even on a full-time job may not be feasible. In September 1997 the minimum wage was raised to $5.15/hour. Assume that a low-skilled worker has a job making $6/hour, or slightly above the minimum wage. Say that this worker works 2,080 hours a year, which is forty hours per week, fifty-two weeks per year. Total earnings for this worker would be $12,480, which is slightly below the official poverty level for a family of three, and substantially below the poverty level for a family of four or more. Thus in the absence of any government assistance, even a full-time job may not be enough to support a family at the poverty line—much less to offer that family any genuine hope of moving above the poverty line. In addition, most of the families who remain poor do not have steady employment. A much more typical pattern is periods of work followed by periods of joblessness. In 1993 only about a quarter of single mothers and three-quarters of married fathers with a high school degree or less actually earned enough after taxes to move a family with two children out of poverty. However, their low earnings reflected not just their low wages, but also their less than full-time work.

One obvious policy proposal is to raise the minimum wage further. Indeed, grassroots groups across the country have marched under the banner of a "living wage," proposing that states or cities should consider raising the minimum wage to assure that people with a full-time job will be able to support a family. For example, if a single wage earner is to support a family of four, then a minimum wage of nearly $8/hour would be necessary to reach the poverty line.

There are three broad arguments against using the minimum wage as the primary tool for assisting the working poor. First, a higher minimum wage may discourage employers from hiring low-skilled workers, and thus raise the unemployment rate among the very group one wants to help. A typical estimate from the research literature is that raising the minimum wage by 10 percent would decrease employment among low-skilled workers by perhaps 2–3 percent with most of the effects concentrated among teenagers. A second argument is that the minimum wage is insufficiently focused on the poor families that are the source of concern. Many minimum wage workers are teenagers or second earners in families with adequate incomes. Of the 6.2 million workers who were paid at or below $5.15/hour in 1997, about 30 percent were sixteen to nineteen years old. One study found that of the increase in wages from a minimum wage, about half flows to families with incomes of twice the poverty level or more. A third difficulty with the minimum wage is that even a substantially higher minimum wage will still not pay enough to allow an escape from poverty for workers with large families.

Proponents of raising the minimum wage note that any adverse impacts on employment are rather small. Say that the minimum wage goes up 10 percent, and employment falls by 2–3 percent among low-skilled workers. The upside is higher wages for the other 97–98 percent of low-skilled workers. A rise of 10 percent in the current level of the minimum wage would mean an extra $1,000 for a full-time worker. For a household near the poverty line, this is a raise of no small importance.

But supporters of a higher minimum wage don't stop there. They have offered a new wave of somewhat controversial studies suggesting that modest increases in the minimum wage have no adverse effects on employment. For example, one study by economists Alan Krueger and David Card of Princeton University found that workers in fast food restaurants in New Jersey suffered no more unemployment than a comparable group in Pennsylvania after New Jersey raised its minimum wage. Although this study has not gone unchallenged, it has influenced the public debate on this issue.

Rather than requiring employers to pay a substantially higher minimum wage, a better alternative is to have the government pay wage subsidies directly to workers. The Earned Income Tax Credit is currently the main vehicle for doing so. Workers in low-income families receive a refundable tax credit that increases with the income that they earn and the number of children in the family. For example, in 1998, for a family with two or more children, the EITC paid forty cents for every dollar earned up to a maximum credit of $3,756 at an income level of $9,390. (The credit is less generous for families with only one child and provides only minimal support to those without children.) The credit begins to phase out at incomes of $12,260 and disappears entirely at incomes above $30,095. About 20 million workers claimed the EITC in 1998, receiving an average of about $1,600. The EITC is now the single largest antipoverty program funded by the federal government, costing about $30 billion in 1998. A minimum wage worker with two children who earns about $10,000 a year can, with the help of the EITC and food stamps, move slightly above the poverty line. According to the President's Council of Economic Advisers, about half the decline in child poverty between 1993 and 1997 was due to the greater generosity of the EITC.

The EITC has several substantial advantages over raising the minimum wage. Since the EITC is paid by the U.S. Treasury directly to workers, rather than by employers, it offers no incentive for the employer to lay off or hire fewer low-wage workers. Since it is filed with one's taxes, it can be adjusted for the size of a household or the presence of children. It increases automatically with the number of hours worked, and thus provides an incentive to work at the low end of the wage scale.

On the flip side, the EITC has four well-publicized difficulties. First, it can be claimed fraudulently by people who misreport their income. It is the only place in the tax system where it can pay to claim that you have *more* income than you actually have! Second, since it is usually paid as a part of income tax refunds, it arrives all at once, rather than being spread throughout the year so that poor families can use it to pay for rent and groceries. (It is legally possible for employers to provide "negative withholding"—that is, to raise what workers are paid now and then have the employer receive the tax credit from the government later—but it has been difficult to induce employers to participate in this effort.) Third, because the amount of assistance received is tied to total earnings rather than to hourly wages, some of the benefits go to higher-wage workers who spend few hours in the workforce. Fourth, although the EITC encourages work effort by very low-income workers, it is phased out once income reaches a certain level. In the range where workers lose some of the EITC for every hour of extra effort, it discourages additional work. As the credit is presently structured, many more workers are in the phase-out range than in the range where work is encouraged. None of these problems with the EITC is insurmountable, but solving them requires potentially costly administrative and enforcement efforts.

For these and other reasons, some analysts would prefer arranging a subsidy paid through employers. For example, Edmund Phelps of Columbia University would like to see the EITC replaced with a wage rate subsidy, which would focus on raising hourly wages paid rather than annual income. For example, employers hiring someone now earning $6 an hour might receive a subsidy equal to $1 per hour. The subsidy would encourage employers to raise the wages of eligible workers by the amount of the subsidy because at that point the net (after-subsidy) cost to the employer would be no higher than before, and employers who tried to keep the subsidy and avoid raising wages would quickly be outbid by employers who were willing to pass the subsidy along. An alternative approach is to subsidize temporarily employers who hire low-skilled employees. The Work Opportunity Tax Credit provides a targeted tax cut for hiring individuals from groups that have high unemployment rates (or other special needs). The tax credit can pay up to 40 percent of wages, under certain conditions, for hiring a recipient of TANF or food stamp benefits, as well as other designated groups like ex-veterans and ex-felons.

However, wage subsidies passed through employers create paperwork burdens for firms, may stigmatize eligible workers in ways that make employers less rather than more willing to hire them, and may not be cost-effective or politically palatable if they end up subsidizing the private sector for hiring workers they would have hired anyway. Anecdotes from the chief tax executives in large companies suggest that they scour their records after the tax year is over to see if they accidentally hired anyone eligible for the Work Opportunity Tax Credit.

A number of states have experimented in recent years with allowing AFDC recipients to keep a portion of their welfare check when they go to work, to provide an additional incentive for work effort. Similarly, the Canadian government is experimenting in two provinces with an extremely generous earnings supplements program to those who forgo welfare and commit to full-time work. Evaluations of these experiments suggest that such programs increase the earnings and employment of the poor, with an earnings gain to participants that is about triple the cost to the government. The most successful programs in the United States appear to be those that combine the carrot of an earnings subsidy with the stick of a work requirement, so that less skilled individuals are both pushed and pulled into the job market.

Yet another alternative for assisting the working poor is to go beyond thinking about cash in people's pockets and to consider instead subsidizing expenditures on certain necessities such as medical care, food, and child care. If a single parent takes a job, the net gain in actual spendable family income will be the amount earned, minus any additional costs of child care and health care and any loss in other benefits such as food stamps, housing assistance, and the Earned Income Tax Credit. Very often, the loss of such benefits discourages work by low-income people to a much greater extent than would the highest income tax rates faced by the most affluent members of society.

With respect to health care, the major problem is now among adults rather than children. In a quiet revolution, largely unnoticed outside of policy circles, a process of expanding medical assistance to poor children has already occurred. Under current law, all poor children born after 1983, and some children with incomes as high as 185 percent of poverty, are eligible for Medicaid. Congress further expanded funding for children's health care under the State Children's Health Insurance Program (S-CHIP) enacted in 1997. This program provides $24 billion in federal funding to states over five years to expand health insurance programs for uninsured children in families with incomes below 200 percent of the poverty level. Among adults, those eligible to receive welfare under the old AFDC program are also eligible for Medicaid, but if such an individual takes a job with no health coverage, the person may lose this assistance. Thus the group now least likely to have health insurance is low-paid adults working for small employers.

Food is another area in which government has decided to provide noncash assistance to the poor by giving them food stamps, or coupons that can be used to purchase food. Until 1996 food stamps provided assistance to poor households regardless of household composition or other circumstances. As a result of changes to the program in 1996, able-bodied adults without dependents face work requirements or time limits, and many immigrants are ineligible. The food stamp program is quite widespread; in fact, 25 million people received food stamps in 1996, while only 12 million received welfare through AFDC. Moreover, overall federal spending on food stamp benefits in 1996 was $23 billion, which is about what the federal and state governments combined spent on welfare payments in that year. In states that have set their welfare payments at quite low levels, food stamps may actually be worth double or more the amount of the welfare check.

Child care represents yet another cost that may make work difficult for poor parents. If a single mother, earning low wages, does not have trustworthy or affordable child care, she may well end up feeling that it makes more sense to stay home, even if it means being dependent on welfare and food stamps. Child care costs families who pay for it between $4,000 and $5,000 a year for one preschool-age child, making it unaffordable when one is earning poverty level wages. Although child care subsidies have expanded rapidly in recent years and are available to many families, especially those making the transition from welfare to work, a 1997 estimate suggests that only about one in eight of the lower-income children eligible to receive help through the government's main block grant program is receiving such assistance (typically in the form of a voucher that can be used to pay any state approved provider as well as a relative). Further, most states give preference for limited day care slots to parents moving off the welfare rolls at the expense of those who may be equally needy but who have no ties to the welfare system. If the government were to offer poor parents additional help with paying for child care, it would make it easier for these parents to work and simultaneously increase their spendable incomes. High-quality programs with a more educationally oriented curriculum, such as Head Start, could also help to prepare their children for school.

In thinking about assisting the poor and the working poor, it's important to remember that there is unlikely to be any single magic bullet that will address their problems. Instead, the public policy task is to consider some combination of policies, including the minimum wage; wage subsidies, whether from the government directly or through employers; noncash benefits like Medicaid, food stamps, and child care; work requirements, training, and job search programs; as well as rent subsidies and other kinds of public assistance not discussed here.

It is also worth pointing out that funds to defray some of the costs of greater assistance for the working poor currently exist. States continue to receive the same amount of money from the

TANF block grant, regardless of the size of their caseloads. But because these caseloads have declined dramatically since 1996, they currently have excess funds to devote to the working poor if they so choose. They could now experiment with an investment in job training, in child care, or in a state financed EITC, for example.

Redistributing Income from the Rich

The very upper end of the income distribution has done very well indeed in the last twenty years. In 1996 111,000 households in the U.S. filed tax returns reporting more than $1 million in income for the year—and another 214,000 households reported income of between $500,000 and $1 million for the year. Moreover, the well-to-do are more likely to own stocks, and so they have disproportionately benefited from the resurgent stock market boom of the 1980s and 1990s. Given the extraordinary good fortune of the well-to-do, good fortune that has fed upon itself and multiplied in the 1990s stock market, is there a case for having the rich pay a greater share of the tax burden?

One immediate response is that the well-to-do are already paying a greater share of the tax burden. The discussion in chapter 2 pointed out that one of the key elements of Bill Clinton's 1993 budget balancing plan was higher tax rates on the wealthy. Moreover, the reason why the federal budget picture shifted so quickly, from expecting a string of deficits to expecting a string of surpluses, was that tax receipts were very much higher than expected in the late 1990s. The lion's share of that increase in tax receipts has come from those well-to-do households who are earning more income and cashing in some of their stock market gains, while taxes paid by the bottom 80 percent of the income distribution have not changed much.

Contrary to popular belief, the typical rich person does not avoid paying taxes. In 1995 households earning $40,000 per year paid about 10 percent of their income in federal income tax; those with incomes of $100,000 paid about 17 percent; and those with $1 million or more paid 31 percent. In that same year, the top 1.2 percent of all households (those reporting more than $200,000) paid 32 percent of total income taxes collected. The income of the very rich has continued to rise at a very rapid rate. Preliminary data for 1997 suggest that those with income over $200,000 now constitute 1.5 percent of all taxpayers, receive about 20 percent of all adjusted gross income, and pay 37 percent of the total income tax bill.

The high proportion of taxes paid by the wealthy results both because they have a very large share of total income and because the share of income paid in taxes rises as income rises. The current degree of progressivity built into the income tax rate structure (that is, the extent to which tax rates rise with income) is a little more than in the 1980s, but the income tax is much less progressive than in the 1950s, 1960s, and 1970s. However, the structure of tax rates doesn't tell the entire story. The Tax Reform Act of 1986 significantly lowered the top tax rate but also eliminated many of the tax loopholes previously enjoyed by the rich. The changes were designed to have a minimal effect on the total tax burden and its distribution. Also, personal income taxes don't include either the federal payroll taxes that finance Social Security and Medicare or any state and local taxes. These taxes have grown enormously relative to federal taxes on income. As a result, the typical middle class family now pays more in payroll than in income taxes. According to a recent study by the Congressional Budget Office, the federal tax system as a whole became considerably less progressive between 1980 and 1985 as income taxes were cut significantly, but rapidly became more progressive again between 1985 and 1995. Between 1995 and 1999 there was no significant change in the degree of progressivity, and the system today is only slightly more progressive than it was in 1980.

The fairness of taxes, like some forms of beauty, is very much in the eye of the beholder. When it comes to taxing the rich, the issues are both ethical and practical. In ethical terms, there is a legitimate and difficult question about what is a fair distribution of society's resources, on the one hand, and what is the maximum share of anyone's income that the state should be allowed to command, on the other. In practical terms, how much do high marginal tax rates on the rich reduce their work effort, saving, and entrepreneurship, and thus injure the economy as a whole? An additional practical question is the extent to which higher tax rates set off such an intense search for legal tax loopholes and illegal tax evasion that they result in only a negligible increase in tax revenues received by the government.

The problems caused by high tax rates—like discouraging productive economic effort and encouraging activities to evade taxes—can be lessened, while still collecting the same overall level of revenues, if the tax base is "broadened," which means eliminating tax loopholes and using the resulting revenue to keep tax rates lower than they otherwise would be. Of course, one person's tax loophole is another's legitimate economic incentive. A number of important special provisions in the tax code, such as tax exempt interest from municipal bonds and the deductions for interest paid on a home mortgage and for charitable contributions, had sufficient political staying power to survive the Tax Reform Act of 1986. Such popular provisions will not easily be curbed or eliminated by any future reform.

There are two broad sorts of proposals for raising taxes on the wealthy. A first proposal is to raise tax rates on the top incomes, say, on those earning more than $200,000 per year. But many of these households are already paying 40 percent of their marginal dollar earned in federal income taxes. When state and local income and sales taxes are figured into the mix, many are paying half of any additional money earned to some level of government.

The rich have at least two perfectly legal ways to reduce the income taxes that they pay. One is to work less, and thus to earn less money. This effect can be especially prominent for two-earner couples, where it doesn't feel worthwhile for the second earner to take a job if the income received will be taxed at a rate of 50 percent or higher, and for the self-employed, including many professionals, who can easily control their work effort.

A second approach is to take advantage of provisions in the tax code that will reduce taxes. For example, the rich can invest in state and local bonds, which are exempt from federal income tax. They can also figure out ways for income to be earned in the form of capital gains, on which tax will need to be paid eventually, but not this year, and which in case of death can be passed along to heirs without any tax being paid at all. Armies of tax lawyers and accountants work night and day to find techniques for avoiding taxes, and as marginal tax rates increase, it becomes more worthwhile for high-income people to pay fees to such tax advisers.

These effects are significant. Back in the early 1960s the top marginal tax rate was 91 percent. In the early 1980s it was 70 percent. But the share of income taxes paid by the very wealthy was not substantially higher in those times than it was during most of the 1990s since ways were found to get around those high tax rates. Conversely, the higher overall level of tax revenues collected from the rich in the late 1990s was primarily the result of economic forces like higher income and the stock market boom, not higher tax rates on the rich. There is no consensus on how high the tax rate must go before it significantly discourages tax-generating economic activity, and thus becomes counterproductive. Tax rates on the very rich, and even on the simply affluent, probably could be raised somewhat. But the lesson of history is that dramatically higher tax rates provoke a counterreaction and will in the end not succeed in collecting nearly as much more in taxes as might have been expected.

A second proposal would tax the wealth of the rich, not their annual income. The primary federal wealth tax is the estate and gift tax, which is imposed at time of death. The estate tax is imposed only on those who leave an estate of more than $625,000, a floor that is presently scheduled to rise to $1 million by the year 2006. The rate of the tax ranges from 18 percent on the first $10,000 of taxable estate up to a maximum rate of 55 percent for taxable estates of over $3 million. In 1997 the tax raised about $20 billion, which was 1.3 percent of all federal tax receipts. The estate tax is accompanied by a gift tax, so that the tax cannot be easily side-stepped simply by giving large chunks of one's money away before death. The gift tax brought in another $2 billion or so.

Nothing very terrible is likely to happen if the estate and gift tax is increased moderately, for example, if the floor of $625,000 was *not* raised to $1 million. But the tax is more likely to be lowered or eliminated than raised, because it is extremely unpopular with small business people and farmers who would like to leave their businesses to their children. It is alleged that such businesses often have to be sold to non-family members to come up with the cash to pay the estate taxes. Perhaps a more serious problem with the tax is that it is so porous. Although a number of the loopholes, such as generation-skipping trusts, have been tightened in recent years, the estate tax still seems to place its main burden on those not fore-sighted enough to hire lawyers to do their estate planning. If the current estate tax is retained, it is worth subjecting it to careful scrutiny and reform to make it more equitable.

The potential harm done to the economy by higher taxes on the rich is often exaggerated, but there are solid, hard-headed reasons not to push too hard. Pushing income or estate tax rates too high will create unwelcome disincentives to work and save, and will not raise as much revenue as expected.

Few politicians in recent years have campaigned for higher taxes of any sort, including taxes focused on the rich. Proposals to reduce income taxes across the board and to scale back or eliminate estate taxes have been more typical. Commonly heard arguments are that the average family is paying too much in taxes and that tax revenues as a proportion of GDP are at an all-time high. But as noted in chapter 2, the average family at any particular income level is not paying more in income taxes than in the past.

Taxes have risen as a proportion of GDP primarily because the income of the very rich has soared. Much of the increase is related to the stock market. Capital gains realizations have risen markedly since the early 1990s. Bonuses for top corporate management and on Wall Street have been remarkable, and taxable withdrawals from special savings accounts like Individual Retirement Accounts and 401ks have been much higher than they would have been in a less bullish stock market. According to the Congressional Budget Office, families in the middle one-fifth of the income distribution are pay-ing about 20 percent or a little less of their income in federal taxes, and this proportion hasn't changed much in recent decades. Whether this level is too high or low will continue to be debated, but with the economy performing so well, there is not much public sen-timent for changing taxes in either direction.

Building an Opportunity Society

After the success of the civil rights movement in reducing the legal and social barriers faced by African-Americans, and the suc-cess of the women's liberation movement in reducing the barriers faced by women, America at the end of the twentieth century is more a land of equal opportunity than at any time in its history. This doesn't mean that family background or society's attitudes toward race and gender no longer matter, but instead that people's lives are shaped more heavily than in the past by their own skills and choices, rather than by their race or gender or family background. Historical research suggests that intergenerational mobility in the United States has been increasing for decades—perhaps even since the middle of the nineteenth century.

The extent of opportunity and mobility matters a great deal. One reason that Americans do not seem to be deeply troubled by the rise in inequality from the 1970s to the early 1990s, and why Americans are not stampeding en masse to vote that income be redistributed from rich to poor, is a broad public belief that the fortunes made by people like Bill Gates of Microsoft or Sam Walton of Wal-Mart represent their ability to take advantage of opportunities that were broadly open to everyone, rather than happening because of their wealthy parents or political connections. To many Americans, the extent of inequality isn't as important as whether the economic process that generates that outcome is perceived to be fair.

However, the widening income gaps in recent decades could translate into less opportunity and mobility in the future. America has loosened the gravitational influence of family status and income, and diminished biases concerning gender and race, but because the economy of the future promises to run on the basis of information and technology, education is becoming ever more important to economic success. If the children of the poor have a greater tendency to come from broken families, to get a slow start in the early grades, to perform less well in high school, and to miss out almost entirely on education beyond this level, while the children of more affluent parents experience the opposite pattern, then we may be entering a time when intergenerational mobility will stagnate or decrease rather than expand, and a time when certain children are destined before they reach puberty to be also-rans in the competitive labor market. Research by Isabel Sawhill of the Brookings Institution suggests that precisely such a bifurcation in children's prospects is occurring.

Building an opportunity society starts with strong families: perhaps nothing is as important to a child's development as having concerned, involved parents who have finished school and obtained regular work before starting a family. Having two parents is better for the child than one. Much of the increase in poverty and inequality in recent decades resulted from the growth of single-parent families, as noted earlier. No public policy can substitute for raising a child in a home with two adults who are adequately educated and mature enough to be good parents.

To be sure, declining earnings among less-skilled men may be partly to blame for the deterioration in family life for low-income households. Lifting the income of the working poor through some of the policies discussed earlier in this chapter could reduce stress in those families, and make it somewhat easier for resources of money, time, and attention to reach the children. It is also important to think through the incentives that various programs provide for marriage. For example, under the current Earned Income Tax Credit, a mother with a minimum wage job who marries another low-wage worker will find that her husband's income is counted as part of the household's income, and that the amount received from the EITC may decrease by as much as $1,700. Thus the personal and economic gains from marrying are partly offset by a loss of EITC income as well as a loss of other means-tested benefits.

Despite the undoubted importance of family inputs and attention in helping children, social scientists and policy makers have had to face the humbling fact that government policy is typically not the most important determinant of family behaviors and patterns. These patterns develop as the result of social norms within communities, and are countered or reinforced by everything from media images to churches, from peer pressures to civic programs. The truth is that we don't know how, with a few government grants or tax credits, to strengthen families substantially. As a result, much of the opportunity agenda focuses on how policy might affect children more directly.

Children form patterns of learning and relating to others early, certainly before high school, often even before kindergarten. Thus one cornerstone of the opportunity society is to try to assure that each child gets off to a strong start. These early childhood intervention programs are often generically referred to as Head Start, which is the name of a particular government program. Decades of social science experimentation with such programs have produced two clear lessons.

First, the main benefit of such programs does not seem to come through permanently higher IQ scores or grades in later years. Instead, it seems to come through a greater feeling of attachment to school and a greater ability to adapt to the norms of society. These factors, in turn, lead to more years of school completed and a greater chance of graduating from high school, higher earnings, a reduced likelihood of criminal behavior, and a lower chance of ending up on welfare. Along these dimensions, the returns to programs of early childhood intervention are very much worth the costs.

A second lesson is that the success of any given program is linked to how many resources go into it, assuming the resources are used efficiently. For example, some of the most successful early childhood intervention programs start very early (before age three), employ well-trained professionals, and provide an educationally rich curriculum and an array of other services. In contrast, many of the present Head Start programs have lower-paid staff, only part-time classes for children, and no more than one year of enrollment, typically at age four. Moreover, these programs only serve about 40 percent of all poor children at a time when many four year olds from more affluent families are enrolled in high-quality preschool programs. Thus the children who really need a head start are not always the ones who are getting it.

Early childhood intervention is only the beginning, of course; it should then be reinforced by an improved K-12 schooling system. The economic benefits of better schooling were discussed earlier in chapter 3 as part of an agenda for improved productivity growth. What we want to emphasize here is the importance of education to the opportunity agenda as well. Education has always been the route to upward mobility, the way in which children born into disadvantaged families could climb the economic ladder. But when the education system is weak, the way up is blocked. More than half of fourth and eighth graders in urban public schools fail to meet even minimal standards in reading, math, and science, and more than half of students in big cities will fail to graduate from high school.

Reform of K-12 education is a critical item on the opportunity agenda. But while everyone favors the idea of better schools, it's not altogether clear how to accomplish that goal. A considerable body of economic research has argued that in education, money doesn't necessarily buy better results. For example, over the last few decades, while SAT scores have been flat, per student spending on education has steadily risen about 3 percent per year, average student-teacher ratios have dropped by 22 percent, and the percentage of teachers with a master's degree almost doubled. A number of states with very high levels of education spending per student, like New Jersey and New York, do not seem to produce better students than schools with moderate levels of spending, like Minnesota. Meanwhile, it has been true for decades that a number of inner city parochial and private schools are producing students who are drawn from the same socioeconomic group as their peers in the nearby public schools, and who learn as much or more, but often at much lower cost.

Although many experts in educational reform have come to believe that money is not the key ingredient to improving the performance of schools, this should be understood as an indictment of how that money is currently being spent, not as a rationalization for underfinancing the schools. The hard policy question is how to encourage schools to perform better.

Many believe that America should have national standards to guide what children should know and some means of assessing what they have actually learned. These standards and assessments would provide a benchmark against which to measure performance. Most European countries outperform the United States educationally, and one important reason is probably because they rely on curriculum based external exams to which real consequences attach for students, schools, and teachers. Many states have now established standards and are experimenting with various forms of accountability within the existing school system.

Another currently popular reform is to reduce class size. Many parents feel at a gut level that smaller class sizes are important. One recent experiment in Tennessee found that children who were assigned to smaller classes of about fifteen in kindergarten through third grade performed better academically, even after they were returned to regular-sized classes in the fourth grade. However, critics of this policy point out that many countries, like Japan, have far larger class sizes than the United States but do not seem to have a problem educating their students to a much higher level of proficiency. Moreover, reducing class size substantially and across the board means hiring many more teachers. Such a policy will cost a lot but may not produce corresponding high gains. Most of the benefits of smaller classes accrue to very young children and to those who come from disadvantaged families. Moreover, study after study has shown that the most important factor affecting what children learn is the quality of the teachers. If hiring more teachers ends up diluting the quality of the teaching staff, because the new teachers have less experience, then smaller class sizes could be counterproductive. Schools that are already low performing may be especially susceptible to ending up with a disproportionately large share of the less experienced teachers. If funding for smaller class sizes is spread thinly across all grade levels and school districts, it is unlikely to have much effect.

Others would shake up the structure of school systems by giving parents a greater choice of schools. Choice can take one of three forms: allowing parents to select from among existing public schools, either within a district or statewide; allowing new so-called charter schools to be formed within the public sector; and allowing parents to use publicly funded vouchers to send their children to private schools.

Public school choice is not especially controversial. Some studies suggest that it improves the performance of individual schools who know that they may lose students if they can't compete with other schools in their district or state.

Charter schools are newer and more controversial. By the fall of 1998 thirty-four states and the District of Columbia had enacted school charter laws under which nonprofit organizations, private firms, teachers, or other groups can open a school and compete for students. These schools have to be certified by the state but are freed from many regulations in return for a commitment to meet certain standards. They receive state money according to how many students they attract.

Finally, a few states—including Wisconsin, Ohio, and Florida—

are experimenting with vouchers that are targeted on low-income students but can be used at a private school, including religiously affiliated institutions. These voucher experiments have elicited intense controversy. Critics claim that they siphon resources and good students away from the public schools and may resegregate schools along economic, racial, or religious lines. Advocates argue that they introduce a much needed dose of competition into the provision of schooling and provide new and potentially much better educational opportunities for inner city children whose parents cannot now afford to move to the suburbs or enroll their children in private school. Studies to date of the effects of these experiments on children's school experiences and achievement are modestly encouraging, although far from conclusive.

In the end, it may be that there is no magic bullet for educational reform but that a variety of experiments will eventually lead to an improved system that includes a mixture of public and private elements similar to what now exists in higher education.

Ideally, an opportunity agenda should extend into adulthood, with programs for high school dropouts, financial aid for higher education, and government training and retraining programs for adults. While there is something to be said for this agenda of second chances, public resources are scarce, and it will always be easier, cheaper, and more effective to help kids get on the right path early in life than it will be to help twenty year olds go back to high school or forty year olds retrain for new jobs. The single best way to get more college graduates is to have more high school students who are well qualified to proceed to college. America's education problem is not that its colleges and universities need an overhaul. Instead, America's far-ranging system of colleges and universities, from elite institutions to community colleges, is perhaps the best-functioning portion of the nation's educational system. They offer an area of strength on which other parts of society can build.

The later one waits in life, the harder it is to reshape the established patterns of a lifetime. It is little surprise that many of the job training programs that attempt to retrain the least skilled workers at later ages have had limited success. Classroom training that is not linked to specific job skills is especially suspect; if the school system had the person at a younger and more malleable age, for a full decade and more, and failed, then the chances that a six-month or one-year program will turn someone's life around at a later age are slim.

We do not mean to condemn these sorts of second-chance programs. We are supportive of certain plans to help students finish a high school degree or to afford a college education. There is surely room for experimentation with job training programs, and some of them work in particular circumstances. But in the process of promoting mobility, we should not lose sight of the need to help low-skilled workers in a direct and measurable way by boosting their income, as argued earlier in this chapter. It is neither cost-effective nor humane to offer short-term training programs that provide few skills or skills for which there may be no demand.

Conclusion

The twenty-first century promises to be a time of extraordinary opportunities. New industries, as yet seen only through a mist of uncertainty, will emerge. New jobs, requiring skills and qualifications that do not yet exist, will be created. New products, as yet undreamt of, will become commonplace. As society becomes wealthier, the possibilities for expanding the horizons of the human experience through travel, education, and entertainment will become even broader. Many of the children born in this decade will see almost all of the twenty-first century, and the world in which they live will quite probably change just as much as the world of those who were born between 1900 and 1910 and lived until the 1990s.

The details of this future of opportunity and promise can be seen only hazily, through a clouded crystal ball. But we do have one insight that seems unlikely to be changed by events: without a solid educational background, starting in early childhood, the best of these jobs and experiences will be out of reach for many children before they are even old enough to vote.

5

The Unavoidable Necessity
of Renegotiating the
Intergenerational Compact

Through most of human history, few people retired. Prior to the nineteenth century, most people worked until they dropped, and if they were not dead when they dropped, they could often expect to be treated miserably. Traditionally, children helped support their parents, but the level of support was typically very low. In the United States, this situation improved significantly in the late nineteenth century. Civil War pensions represented an early form of Social Security, in that a very large portion of the population qualified for them. Those pensions began to be complemented at about that time by an array of other support mechanisms, including assistance from trade unions, fraternal orders, charities, and local governments. Shortly after the turn of the century, corporate pensions became more common, and through it all, adult children continued to be a significant source of support for the elderly as well. Saving for one's own retirement was not common. Only the affluent and a few of the successfully self-employed provided for their own retirement.

The support system for the elderly that had evolved after the Civil War could not survive the ravages of the Great Depression. When the Great Depression hit the United States, the elderly suffered along with everyone else, but their adult children suffered twice: once because their own economic prospects had declined, and a second time because they were expected to provide additional support for parents. The immediate and extraordinary popularity of Social Security among all age groups, not just the elderly, is surely based in part on the reality that many people prefer to pay a fixed payroll tax and have the government send their elderly parents a check rather than feel a responsibility of sending a regular check to their parents directly and dealing with the attendant negotiations and familial pressures. Moreover, during the Great Depression, Social Security offered a promise that some of the elderly would leave the labor force, and that their jobs would thus be available to others. Thus from its very beginning Social Security was intertwined with other social goals beyond assuring a basic standard of living to the elderly, like easing the burden on adult children and reducing the labor force participation of the elderly.

Although the Great Depression provided the catalyst for the formation of the Social Security system, it is doubtful that the traditional support system could have adjusted to growing life expectancies in the longer run. It is one thing to expect children to support their parents for a few years; it is quite another to expect that support to last for one or two decades, or more.

In any case, Social Security socialized the implicit compact between parents and their children. The risk faced earlier by adult children, that their parents might live longer than expected, and the risk faced by retirees, that economic fluctuations might reduce the stream of family income available to them, were collectivized. But no one foresaw the remarkable swings in birth rates experienced in the forty years following the founding of Social Security. Birth rates first soared and produced the baby boom generation between the end of World War II and the early 1960s. From 1929–1946 the U.S. population increased from 122 million to 142 million, a rise of just under 1 percent per year. Over the next seventeen years, from 1946 to 1963, the population increased from 142 million to 189 million, a rise of about 2 percent per year. Fertility then plummeted and has remained at a low level ever since. In the thirty-five years from 1963 to 1998 the population rose from 189 million to 270 million, an average increase of just more than 1 percent per year.

These population growth figures were reflected in fertility rates: the number of children born to the average woman rose from 2.3 children/woman in 1940 to 3.8 children/woman at the peak of the baby boom in 1957. Today, the fertility rate has declined back to 2.0 children/woman.

The difference between 2 percent and 1 percent annual rates of population growth, or between 2.3 and 3.8 children per woman, may not seem huge, but when compounded over more than a decade these changes add up to dramatic social shifts. A baby boom followed by a baby bust creates the worst possible situation for programs such as Social Security that rely on taxing present day workers to finance payments to the retired population.

As the baby boom generation approaches retirement—those born in 1946 will turn sixty-five in 2011—life expectancy continues to increase, which raises further the proportion of elderly in the population. In 1997 life expectancy at birth for men was 72.9 years; for women, it was 79.3 years. By 2030 male life expectancy is projected by the actuaries at the Social Security Administration (SSA) to rise 3.6 years, to 76.5 years, while female life expectancy will have risen by 2.4 years, to 81.7 years. While these estimates are the "intermediate" projections of the SSA, some demographers are concerned that these estimates may be too pessimistic—that is, that life expectancy will actually rise more rapidly. The SSA estimates are based on an underlying premise that the gains in life expectancy that have occurred over the twentieth century will slow down in the first few decades of the twenty-first century. However, in other developed economies that have longer life expectancies than the United States—for example, the United Kingdom, Sweden, France, and Japan—no such slowdown has been observed.

The combination of the boomer generation and growing life expectancies will mean a graying of America; that is, the proportion of Americans over the age of sixty-five will rise. Fifty years ago, one out of twelve Americans was over the age of sixty-five. The figure is now one in eight. By 2030 the demographic projections are that one in five Americans will be over the age of sixty-five.

Another way of viewing the problem asks how many workers are available to support each Social Security beneficiary. In 1960 the ratio of payroll tax paying workers to beneficiaries was 5.1. By 1999 the ratio had sunk to 3.4. The ratio is expected to fall to 2.1 workers per beneficiary by 2030!

Anticipating the Shape of the U.S. Economy as America Turns Gray

This shift in the age distribution of the U.S. population toward the elderly will have a wide range of consequences. From 2010 to 2030 the number of people over the age of sixty-five will rise by 70 percent, while the number from twenty to sixty-four will rise just 4 percent. Family patterns will inevitably shift. The extended four-generation family—that is, children, parents, grandparents, and great-grandparents—is becoming well known now; by 2030 it may be almost commonplace. The ties of affection, attention, support, time, and money between these generations will be increasingly complex as new patterns emerge.

In thinking about flows of money from older to younger, for example, it was one thing for a person dying at age seventy to leave her money to her son who was age forty, with a few children soon heading to college. The situation is quite different for a person dying at ninety to think about leaving money to a son who is about to retire at age sixty, and who has a granddaughter who is thinking about taking a few years out of the workforce to have children at age thirty. In thinking about resource flows in the other direction, from younger to older, adult children may find that looking after an elderly parent who lives to seventy-five is quite a bit different—fifteen years different, in fact—from looking after an elderly parent who lives to age ninety. Again, stories of those who have just retired looking after their still-living parents are heard with some regularity now; by 2030 that situation may be so common as to require barely any comment. The question may soon be to what extent the adult *grandchildren*, having reached their thirties and forties, should spend time and attention and money supporting their grandparents—or even to the relationships that will develop between some great-grandchildren in their twenties and great-grandparents in their nineties! In a large country with easy movement, and an economy where careers come and go, some family members will often end up living scattered far apart while others remain nearby, which will only complicate these family relationships further.

The growing number of elderly will have other effects as well. For example, it may transform the volunteer sector of the economy. A 1996 survey showed that nearly 45 percent of the population over the age of fifty-five, and 34 percent of the population over age seventy-five, volunteer at least several hours a week on a regular basis. In turn, a growing number of volunteers has wide-ranging implications for education, religion, child care, health care, home support, cleanup of parks, neighborhood groups, assistance to the poor, libraries, and many other tasks and relationships.

Patterns of aggregate economic growth will be profoundly affected as the ratio of retirees to workers climbs after 2010. Remember, current projections from 2010 to 2030 forecast almost zero growth in the U.S. workforce for the first time in U.S. economic history. As the baby boomers retire in huge numbers, the nation will lose the production of highly experienced workers. The fear that one sometimes hears today of companies trying to ditch older workers for younger, cheaper ones may become largely a thing of the past—because there will be a shortage of such younger workers. Forward-thinking firms may want to start thinking now about how they will design their personnel policies to encourage older workers to stay on. In particular, "defined benefit" pension plans that guarantee a certain level of retirement payment at a certain age tend to encourage early retirement and may need to be altered so that they encourage longer work. More flexible arrangements may be offered to older workers so that they can work part time at interesting jobs. To make this possible, laws and tax rules that govern retirement and pension funds will have to be altered. Most of these rules are designed on the assumption that sixty-five was the "right" and definite retirement age, and thus they make flexible steps, like offering partial retirement, quite difficult.

The growing proportion of elderly and retirees in the economy after 2010 will lead to a high consumption, low savings economy. Around 2020, on the present path of spending and taxes, government surpluses will be converted into ever-larger deficits as the surplus in the Social Security trust fund first dwindles and then becomes a deficit. As the number of retirees increases, the assets of private pension plans, which have been one of the largest and most reliable contributors to national savings in the last few decades, will start declining in size by about 2020; that is, they will be paying out more to the already retired than they will be taking in from the workforce of that time. The growing number of retirees will to some extent be living off their savings. This pattern raises a number of disturbing questions.

If the level of savings in an economy is low, that typically means that the economy has less capital available for investment. But as pension funds and retirees sell off their stock portfolios, who will buy them? In 2030, when an older person wants to sell off a four-bedroom family house and downsize to a smaller place, how many families with children will be interested in stepping up to buy the larger home at a price close to that originally paid?

The issue of who will buy assets as the retirees sell them off is a difficult one. Perhaps fewer Americans will retire than expected, or they will retire later, and so will continue accumulating assets rather than selling them off. Perhaps the Americans who are working in 2020 will be interested in saving much, much, much more than expected, and they will buy the homes and stocks of the retirees. Perhaps there will be a rise in demand from the Chinese middle class of 2020, buying U.S. stocks over whatever the Internet will be called two or three decades from now. Perhaps most people won't sell their older homes and downsize but will simply continue to live in them. When retirement advisers and long-term financial planners are feeling gloomy, they contemplate the nightmare scenario of how much asset prices might have to fall in the second and third decades of the twenty-first century to induce people to buy the securities that pension funds and retirees and the federal government will want to sell. They also worry about how the retirees of 2030 will react if they find that their houses and stocks and financial investments just don't sell for as much as they had planned and hoped.

It's not clear how this low-saving economy will continue to prosper and grow. To make the situation just a little more difficult, remember that the problem of an aging population is not just an American issue, but a problem faced by all the developed economies of the world. In fact, the ratio of elderly to the working-age population in a number of other countries, like Japan and Italy, will rise more rapidly than in the United States. Thus if one is tempted to say that the U.S. economy can continue to rely on investment capital from abroad, as it had to a large extent in the 1990s, it's important to remember that lower-saving economies all over the developed world will be thinking about relying on capital from abroad—and they won't all be able to succeed.

From a public policy standpoint, of course, the key issues with which the country must grapple as America turns gray are Social Security and health care programs for the elderly. But in thinking about these programs and how they might be amended, it's important to keep in mind that all the issues they raise about work and saving and public programs will be embedded in the context of an economy that might look quite different. The population of elderly beneficiaries will also look very different. For example, many more recipients than today will be divorced or never married. There will be fewer traditional housewives and many more women whose work histories are similar to those of men. Policy solutions designed today must be cut to fit the shape of tomorrow's problems.

Renegotiating Social Security

Social Security socialized many of the risks created by the implicit moral and social contract between the elderly and their children. An adult child no longer faced a special economic burden if a parent lived longer than average, and a retired parent no longer faced the risk that an adult child might become unemployed. In either case, the Social Security benefits just kept coming. But the risks facing individuals are not the same as the systemic risks facing society as a whole. The burden of the financial risk imposed by an individual parent living longer than expected can be spread across society, but society must still deal with the issues created when life expectancy rises for the whole population or when birth rates fall precipitously. "Society" is not a disembodied entity that will magically pay the bills, nor is it a particular group like workers or retirees. Society is all of us.

It seems reasonable to think about renegotiating the contract between the generations. After all, contracts are often renegotiated when economic or other conditions change substantially and un-expectedly. Some of the key parameters defining the Social Secu-rity program as it stands today are provided in Table 2.

TABLE 2. About Social Security
Old Age, Survivors and Disability Insurance

	1998		
Number of Recipients (OASDI)	44,076,000		
Number of Covered Workers	148,459,000		
	Employer	Employee	Self-Employed
Tax Rate (OASDI)	6.2%	6.2%	12.4%
	1997	1998	1999
Tax Base (OASDI)	$65,400	$68,400	$72,600
	Retired Worker	Disabled Worker	
Average Monthly Benefit Amount	$780	$733	
	Trust Fund Status: 1998		
[*in billions of dollars*]	OASI	DI	
Assets at End of 1997	$589.1	$66.4	
Receipts into Trust Fund (1998)	424.8	66.4	
Outgo from Trust Fund (1998)	332.3	49.9	
Net Increase in Assets (1998)	92.5	14.4	
Assets at End of 1998	681.6	80.8	

Sources: The Social Security Administration (SSA). *1999 Trustees Report*
[http://www.ssa.gov/OACT/TRSUM/trsummary.html], and *SSA Fact Sheet*
[http://www.ssa.gov/OACT/FACTS/fs1998__12.html].

In retrospect, it is unfortunate that the nature of Social Security's moral contract was altered fundamentally in the 1970s through au-tomatic indexing of benefit levels to inflation. The program now in-dexes initial benefits so that they rise with wage increases; after retirement, benefits are indexed to the inflation rate and no longer rise in real terms. Prior to indexing, changes in the level of benefits were made at the discretion of the Congress. Over some periods, benefits were allowed to erode in real terms; in other periods, Con-gress overadjusted. Indexing was a response to a series of very large benefit increases implemented in the late 1960s and early 1970s that far exceeded the inflation rate. It was thought at the time that once

Congress opened up the issue of benefit levels it could not restrain itself, especially in election years, and it was better to put the system on automatic pilot. Thus indexing was expected to save money over time.

With the benefit of hindsight, the large discretionary Social Security increases of the late 1960s and early 1970s can be seen as a natural reaction to the extraordinary economic growth rates of the 1960s. At that time, the elderly were an especially poor segment of the population, and society could afford to treat them better. Discretionary benefit increases were not excessive before the late 1960s, in the sense that benefits over time more or less kept pace with rises in the cost of living, and it is doubtful that they would have been excessive during the 1970s, when wages failed to rise as rapidly as inflation. Instead, having Social Security benefits indexed to inflation during the 1970s meant that benefits for the elderly rose more quickly than the wages of the ordinary workers who were paying payroll taxes.

Were indexing for inflation not so firmly in place, Congress could let benefit levels quietly erode by a few percentage points, which could be a considerable help in striking a deal to rebalance the system. However, since economic growth gradually raises wage levels over time, the indexing of initial benefits to wages means that each successive cohort of retirees is promised higher real benefits on average. This promise is a very expensive one, especially when demographic conditions are shifting toward an older population. It has also been a very successful promise, in that the elderly have gone from being one of the poorest segments of the population in the early 1960s to having poverty rates that are lower than the rest of the population. The question is how much pressure should be placed on the working population to keep this system going at promised levels.

Many believe that Social Security works like a bank account: you pay in during your working life, and then Social Security pays you back after retirement. This belief is not true. Instead, Social Security is part of the compact between generations. Today's working-age population supports the elderly and in turn expects to receive benefits based on the taxes collected from the workers of tomorrow. This is called a "pay-as-you-go" system; the alternative, where funds are actually stored up in advance over a worker's lifetime, is called a "funded" system.

A pay-as-you-go system is vulnerable to demographic shifts like the graying of the baby boom generation and longer life expectancies. Such changes mean that the proportion of workers to elderly can alter dramatically, which puts the system under stress. By the 2030s payroll taxes will cover only about 75 percent of the promised benefits for that year and future years.

Optimists sometimes hold out hope that these dire projections will not come to pass. Of course, any such projections are based on a variety of assumptions about economic growth, interest rates, inflation, immigration, life expectancy, and many other factors, and if the assumptions are too pessimistic, then the outcomes will be better than expected. However, the Social Security Administration has historically tended to be somewhat too optimistic; that is, the projections of when the trust fund would run out of money have more often moved closer to the present rather than farther away as further information emerged. While one can pick at any of the individual economic and demographic assumptions, there is little reason to believe that the SSA has been so pessimistic in a majority of its projections that all the worries about Social Security are a cosmic false alarm.

In 1983, staring the expected long-term demographic changes in the face, the structure of Social Security was altered so that it would start building up a surplus in its trust fund. In effect, the program shifted to becoming partially funded. The notion was that the surplus could be accumulated now and then drawn down as the boomers retire. By the late 1990s surpluses were accumulating in the Social Security trust fund at a rate of about $80 billion per year. The total amount in the fund in the year 2000 will be about $800 billion. Although the estimates of future trust fund balances shift a bit each year as the economy evolves, the basic pattern is clear enough. A few years after 2010, soon after the first baby boomer born in 1946 hits age sixty-five, the benefits being paid out of Social Security will exceed the payroll taxes being paid in. However, because of the interest earnings being paid on the past accumulated surpluses, the trust fund will continue to grow for a few years more. The trust fund will peak in size around 2022, at $4.5 trillion. At that time, that amount will be equal to almost three full years of payments. Then the trust fund is gradually drawn down until it is entirely depleted in the 2030s.

The trust fund has been an enormous source of controversy and confusion. It is common to suggest that the Social Security problem will be "solved" if the trust fund can be kept solvent for the next seventy-five years. But the true economic costs imposed by paying Social Security benefits is in no way affected by the financial condition of the trust fund. The costs are better measured by the share of the GDP required to finance benefits, since this captures the share of output that is being spent on Social Security and thus is not available for other social needs. Choosing to run larger surpluses in the trust fund does not, by itself, ease the overall costs of Social Security, either in the present or the future.

If the nation followed the practice of assuring that the trust fund surplus would always function as an addition to the overall federal budget, the situation would be different. Increases in the trust fund surplus would then translate into increases in national saving. Higher national savings would enhance economic growth (as discussed in chapter 3). However, in and of itself, additional economic growth does surprisingly little to address the long-term solvency of Social Security. On the revenue side, growth does increase wages and push up payroll taxes, but on the expenditure side, higher wages also mean higher initial benefit levels. The bottom line is that faster economic growth helps the Social Security outlook a little, but unless it is combined with changes in how initial benefits are indexed to wages, growth is not an especially substantial step toward fixing the system.

The most common proposal for attempting to assure that Social Security would add to national savings is to set up budget rules (or even a constitutional amendment) that would require that the Social Security surplus be taken out of the official budget, and the rest of the budget would have to be balanced. This proposal has a certain populist appeal, but it quickly encounters both practical and theoretical difficulties. The practical problem is that it hasn't worked in the past. For example, Social Security was taken off budget in the early 1990s in an attempt to assure that it would add to budget surpluses, but this did not noticeably reduce the large budget deficits of the early 1990s. Conversely, changes in the projected Social Security trust fund surplus have not been the main factor producing the surprising overall budget surplus in the last few years. It is very difficult to bind the hands of future Congresses so that they will make future budget decisions while completely ignoring the Social Security surpluses.

Moreover, there is no economic justification for an ironclad rule that the overall budget outside of Social Security should be balanced each year, or what would be the same thing, that the overall federal budget surplus should be exactly equal to the Social Security trust fund's surplus. The overall budget surplus could reasonably be larger or smaller in any given year, depending on how much the nation wants to save for the future and depending on whether the economy is in an expansion or in a recession.

The Social Security trust fund serves only one useful purpose. It is an accounting device for tracking whether the payroll tax is yielding sufficient revenues to finance promised benefits. When payroll tax revenues exceed benefit payments, as was true in the 1990s and as will be true in the first decade of the twenty-first century, it might be said that the payroll tax burden is being paid early—and that the system gets credit for this by receiving interest for these early payments. While it is of considerable political importance to know whether the payroll tax is sufficient in the long run to fund the benefits that have been promised, this does not affect the real economic burden imposed by paying benefits. Although it is a good idea to run substantial overall surpluses over the next few years to build up national savings and make it mildly easier to afford the retirement of the baby boomers, this step can be taken regardless of the size of the trust fund.

Financing Social Security benefits with an earmarked payroll tax, rather than out of general tax revenues or government borrowing, has the useful effect of making the cost of the system visible, which has probably restrained the growth of benefits in the past. However, it also create an illusion in which too many people believe that they have already paid for their personal benefits and that they own those benefits. This claim is not true for the average current retiree, who is receiving considerably more in benefits than the sum of his or her payroll tax payments and accumulated interest on those taxes would have provided. But given that the belief that benefits are just returning what a person has paid into the system is widespread, it becomes politically very difficult to reduce benefit levels.

Because of the demographic factors discussed above, the annual cost of promised Social Security benefits will rise, unless changes are made, from slightly below 12 percent of taxable payroll currently to 18 percent and above by the middle of the next century. The current policy battle is over how society should react to this projection. Should benefits be cut back to a level that can be financed by today's payroll tax rates or should taxes be raised? If taxes are raised, should the program continue to rely exclusively or primarily on the payroll tax, or should other taxes be devoted to Social Security? Should the changes take place immediately or be deferred until later? Yet another option is to pay for the higher Social Security benefits through government borrowing. But when the burden of Medicare is added to that of Social Security, borrowing alone cannot provide a feasible answer. Covering the whole burden of public support for the elderly in this manner would imply a government debt that grows much faster than national income and an interest bill on that debt that eventually reaches intolerable levels. As promised benefits grow relative to income, the only real choices are to cut back on promised benefits or to raise taxes on workers.

A First Set of Social Security Proposals: Pay Higher Taxes

The arguments for addressing the issues raised by Social Security with increased taxes are straightforward. Social Security is a promise made, and today's retirees have paid payroll taxes all their lives and made retirement plans with that promise in mind. Changing the promised benefits now, it is argued, would be grossly unfair. Therefore, the solution to Social Security's problems should be to levy additional taxes as necessary. Proposals along these lines would put the burden of adjusting the intergenerational compact on current and future workers, rather than on those who are currently retired or soon to retire.

What magnitude of tax increase would be necessary to fix Social Security? If the needed revenues are generated solely by pay-roll tax rate increases, then as noted above, the payroll rate would steadily rise toward 18 percent. The payroll tax is collected half from employees and half from employers, and this 18 percent rate includes both halves. However, the portion of the payroll tax bur-den imposed formally on the employer is ultimately passed on to the worker in the form of lower wages. Alternatively, if the addi-tional funding for Social Security were to come from outside the present system, it could be covered by about a 15 percent increase in every federal tax.

A more fundamental question is whether the entire burden of adjusting to adverse demographic developments should take the form of tax increases on workers. A strong case can be made for considering a renegotiation of the contract among generations. Promised benefits are not sacrosanct; Congress has adjusted them a number of times over the decades. The political system has made unrealistic promises; surely all sides should share in the cost of ad-justment. It does not seem especially fair that those born into larger generations, like the baby boomers, should be able to pay lower taxes during their working lives because their generation is so nu-merous while the following smaller generation should have to pay higher taxes, again because the baby boomers are so numerous. Why should what a person pays into the nation's retirement system depend on whether the person is born into a large or small gener-ation?

This argument does not necessarily mean, of course, that the whole solution has to come from reduced benefits, either. Taxpay-ers can fairly be asked to share some of the pain. If the payroll tax is increased, it can be done in a number of different ways, although each alternative has trade-offs to consider. For example, the Social Security payroll tax is only paid up to a certain income level. In-stead of raising the payroll tax rate, the upper limit on contributions could be raised. However, this may create a political problem. If the current benefit formula remains unchanged, the upper middle class and the affluent would receive little in the way of benefit increases in return for any increased tax payments. These politically potent groups may then turn against the system. On the other hand, if the benefits of the upper middle class and the affluent are raised, then raising their payroll taxes does little to support the system in the long run. Raising the tax base also creates some potential administrative problems. For example, people who own small businesses often find it easy to avoid tax base increases by converting some of their earnings into a return on capital that is not taxed by the payroll tax. Revenues could also be raised by increasing taxes other than the payroll tax, but this step would certainly reduce the sense of Social Security as a contributory and dedicated system and might make the system more vulnerable to a future wave of tax cut fever.

Additional revenue might also be collected by increasing taxes on Social Security benefits. It is often said that if Social Security benefits were treated like private pensions, 85 percent would be put in the tax base. Under current law, those Social Security recipients with more than $34,000 in other income, if single, or $44,000, if married, must include a portion of their Social Security up to 85 percent of total benefits to be subject to income taxes. However, in recent years private retirement saving has been favored by the tax system in numerous ways like IRA and 401k accounts, tax breaks for retirees selling homes, and so on, and so it is quite misleading to say that 85 percent of all other private pensions are taxable. It would surely not be fair to treat Social Security benefits more harshly than private pensions.

A Second Set of Social Security Proposals: Reduce the Growth in Benefits

In contemplating a cut in promised benefits, it must be remembered that if the economy and wages continue to grow, the current indexing system promises each successive cohort of retirees higher real annual benefits on average. Money could be saved by reducing these projected increases without actually reducing the absolute standard of living of successive generations of retirees. Remember as well that paying each cohort the same absolute real annual benefit on average implies a steady increase in total benefits paid during a lifetime because of growing life expectancy.

A variety of options for reducing the growth in benefits have been suggested. For example, in view of the considerable increases in life expectancy in recent decades, and the further increases that are expected, it may make sense to move back the normal age of retirement. The current normal retirement age is sixty-five, although one can retire as early as sixty-two, at the cost of receiving a correspondingly smaller benefit check. Under current law, the normal retirement age of sixty-five will rise gradually from sixty-five to sixty-six from 2000 to 2005, stay at sixty-six until 2016, then from 2017 to 2022 will gradually rise from sixty-six to sixty-seven. A number of proposals have been made to raise it faster or further, or both.

Pushing back the retirement age is clearly a form of a benefit cut: the benefits that a person would have received at sixty-five or sixty-six will no longer be available until age sixty-seven. If a person still wants to retire at sixty-five, this can be done, but with an annual benefit that is cut by an actuarially fair amount. But this form of a benefit cut by raising the retirement age may make sense, since it reflects growing life expectancies. Sweden has put legislation in place that automatically reduces benefits as life expectancy goes up; the underlying notion is that a person is entitled (on average) to certain benefits, but longer life expectancy means those benefits have to be spread over a greater number of years. Some say that this proposal is unfair to people in physically demanding jobs or in poor health, who may have a greater need to retire earlier. But the ground rules of an all-purpose government retirement program must be set in relation to overall facts about the population, and the actual average age of retirement was higher in the past when people were less healthy, life expectancy was shorter, and physically demanding jobs were much more prevalent.

The notion of a later retirement age is closely linked with the idea that if society encouraged people to work a few years more, it would help the Social Security system. This proposal, of course, runs straight in the opposite direction from one of the original purposes of Social Security, which was to discourage the elderly from working to free up jobs for younger workers.

Currently, Social Security incorporates an "earnings test," which is something of a leftover from the days when the system attempted to encourage older workers to leave the labor force. In 1999 the earnings test had the effect of reducing benefits by $1 for every $3 of earnings above $15,500 a year for workers between the ages of sixty-five and seventy; for early retirees between the ages of sixty-two and sixty-four, the earnings test reduced benefits by $1 for every $2 earned above $9,600. The penalty implied by the earnings test has become less severe over the years, because Social Security has been moving toward a situation in which people who lose benefits because of the earnings test are rewarded later in life by something approaching an actuarially fair increase in benefits. However, considerable empirical evidence suggests that people are more aware of the loss of immediate benefits to the earnings test than they are of the long-term gain in benefits if they work longer. As a result, the earnings test either discourages work or induces older workers to hide their earnings.

Government might attempt a number of different policies to encourage the elderly to work. For example, workers above a certain age—say, seventy or seventy-two—might have Social Security taxes on their earnings reduced. Older workers might be allowed to start drawing on Medicare health benefits while continuing to work, thus reducing their employer's health care costs and providing an incentive for firms to hire older workers. The elderly might receive an Earned Income Tax Credit (parallel to the credit now offered to the poor, discussed in chapter 4), which would give them a tax break that rises up to some point as they earn more income. But before even considering the merits of these substantive proposals, an important first step should be to inform people that the current system already rewards longer work by raising the level of benefits to be received later in life. Once people are better informed regarding the work incentives inherent in the present system, policy makers can assess whether further inducements for the elderly to work are desirable.

As workers become scarce in the early decades of the twenty-first century, market forces may also act to encourage higher labor force participation among the elderly. The wages available to elderly workers should rise, and employers should become more willing to accommodate demands for flexible schedules or part-time work. People are increasingly healthier at older ages. Some will prefer to work, at least part time, partly to enjoy a higher level of consumption and partly because they enjoy a sense of involvement and prestige from their job.

In fact, some evidence from the last few years indicates that a shift may be occurring toward the elderly working more. From the start of Social Security in the 1930s up through the early 1990s, the proportion of men over age sixty-five who were still in the workforce dwindled, falling from 46 percent in 1950 to just 16 percent by the mid-1990s. The proportion of men in the fifty-five to sixty-four age bracket who were still in the workforce dropped as well; it was 87 percent in 1950, but down to 67 percent by the mid-1990s. Men were retiring earlier and earlier. The statistics for women are somewhat different, and show a continued rise in labor force participation, reflecting the fact that women flooded into the paid workforce in the 1970s, and so while most elderly women in earlier generations had not had lifelong careers in the paid workforce, an ever-growing share of women today have had a significant attachment to the paid labor force throughout much of their adult life.

However, in the mid-1990s the proportion of men in the over sixty-five and fifty-five to sixty-four age bracket who were in the labor force has increased slightly. Perhaps this is just a temporary blip due to the strong economy; however, analysts at the Bureau of Labor Statistics expect this trend to continue, at least in a mild way, into the first decade of the twenty-first century. Nevertheless, men are still likely to spend a longer and longer time in retirement because of continuing increases in life expectancy.

An alternative rationale for trimming Social Security benefits is based on the arguments, discussed in some depth in chapter 3, that the measured inflation rate tends to overstate the true amount of inflation, and therefore, indexing benefit levels according to inflation as measured by the Consumer Price Index provides benefits increases that are too high. The primary reason is that it is very difficult to take quality improvements (including those from new goods) into account, and so some price rises that are due to quality improvements are miscounted as inflation.

If the annual rise in Social Security benefits is supposed to reflect the real decline in buying power that happens because of inflation, and the measured inflation rate overstates the true inflation rate, then there is an argument that benefits should be increased each year by, say, the rate of inflation minus 1 percent, or the rate of inflation minus 0.5 percent. Over a year or two, of course, such a change would be barely perceptible. But if a rule of inflation minus I percent were compounded over the next three decades, then benefits at that point would be about 30 percent lower than presently forecast. This step alone would come close to solving the financial imbalance faced by the system. By its nature, it would also phase itself in slowly, allowing time for adjustment. Whatever the rationale for such an action, the bottom line is that benefits would be substantially lower in the future, which makes this a difficult political sell. Moreover, the option would reduce the overall income of poorest retirees by proportionally more than the income of other retirees, because the poorest rely on Social Security benefits for almost all their income. Also, since the Bureau of Labor Statistics has made significant progress in reducing the bias in the CPI, and is poised to make further progress, this option seems less attractive now than it might have a few years ago.

A variety of other benefit cuts are possible, of course. One stealth proposal hidden inside a number of Social Security plans would change the formula for calculating Social Security benefits. Under current law, benefits paid are based on the highest thirty-five years of earnings. If the formula were altered to be based on the highest thirty-eight or forty years of earnings, the additional years would (by definition) be lower-earning years than the years presently included. *Average* annual earnings would be lower, and so would benefits. This proposal also fits with the notion of encouraging people to stay in the workforce longer.

There are also prominent proposals to means-test Social Security benefits, that is, pay lower benefits to those with more outside income. Means-testing sounds fair enough on its face; after all, shouldn't benefit cuts be felt most heavily by those who have other resources? For about 38 percent of elderly households, Social Security benefits make up 80 percent of their income; for 9 percent of elderly households, Social Security benefits are less than 20 percent of their income.

But means-testing has its problems, too. Imagine two people with equal work histories, who make equal Social Security contributions, but one person saves steadily every year, while the other person saves nothing. In such a comparison, it hardly seems fair to reduce Social Security benefits for the saver who reaches retirement with additional resources—and in economic terms, such a policy clearly reduces the incentive for saving. In addition, if the middle class and wealthy started to receive substantially lower Social Security benefits relative to the poor, political support for the system might erode.

A Third Set of Social Security Proposals: Seeking a Higher Return in a Funded Program

The discussion has thus far proceeded as though there is no change in the pay-you-go nature of Social Security. In the present pay-as-you-go system, the implicit return received by Social Security beneficiaries on the past payroll taxes they have paid is adversely affected by any slowdown in the rate of growth of total wages, which would hold down benefit levels, and by any increase in the growth of the number of retirees, which creates political pressures to hold down benefits. One can escape these risks if contributions to the system are saved and invested so that the system is funded. Then the rate of return to contributions is determined by the amount saved and the rate of return to these assets, not by wages or the fluctuating size of succeeding generations. Advocates of such a step also argue that the rate of return for the average retiree could be higher in such a system. However, the present Social Security system redistributes benefits from the rich to the poor, so the "average" return in the present system is a combination of the poor implicit rate of return received by the well-to-do and the quite good implicit rate of return received by those from low-income households.

The biggest hurdle in moving from a pay-as-you-go system to a funded system involves transition costs. Those currently retired cannot be abandoned, and so current workers will have to continue to pay payroll taxes to finance current benefits. However, they will also be expected to reduce their consumption further to make contributions into the accounts that will fund their own future benefits. This transition problem is so severe that it is doubtful that politicians in Washington would be discussing moving toward a funded system were it not for the existence of a substantial federal budget surplus, which could be used to reduce the pain of transition.

There are a variety of approaches to funding Social Security. The current increase in funding could be carried out by government, through collecting higher payroll taxes, or by individuals. In the case of individuals, the contributions can be voluntary and encouraged by tax policy or mandated by government regulation. If government controls the pool of prefunded investment, it can continue to promise a defined benefit similar to that promised by the current system, but government—that is, taxpayers—must then bear the risk that the return on the investment will not be sufficient to fund the benefits that have been promised.

Finance theory teaches that riskier investments involve greater volatility in the short term but then pay higher average returns in the long term to compensate. Thus President Clinton and others have proposed that the Social Security trust fund invest in stocks rather than continuing with present law that requires all of the surplus to be invested in Treasury bonds. Those who favor investing in equities argue that the government is better able to bear the risk of equity investments than are individuals because the government can spread the risk over a number of generations and then benefit from the fact that while stock prices bounce about in the short run, over a time horizon of decades they have paid a considerably higher return than bonds.

Those who oppose having part of the Social Security trust fund invested in stocks typically admit that stocks pay a higher return in the long run but make other counterarguments. They worry that government would use equity investment to achieve political goals, punishing "bad" corporations, like firms that sell tobacco or guns or that have investments in an unpopular country, while rewarding corporate political supporters. Proponents of having the Social Security trust fund invested in equities would set up a structure to insulate the government fund from political pressures, similar to the way the Federal Reserve is sheltered from the hurly-burly of day-to-day politics, but any such structure erected by law could also be eroded or dismantled by a future law. Moreover, skeptics doubt that politicians could resist the temptation to distribute the results of pleasant surprises in the stock market by increasing benefits or reducing contributions immediately, while delaying the effects of unpleasant surprises through borrowing.

An alternative approach to prefunding Social Security would work through individual accounts, which might either work through a government mandating that individuals save in a specified account or by encouraging voluntary saving with tax benefits. Either way, individual accounts would sidestep the political concerns about government involvement in the stock market.

It is difficult to generalize about how individual retirement accounts would work, because significantly different versions have been adopted in various countries, and very different proposals have been put forward in the United States. Basically, individual accounts can be designed to achieve almost any goal held important by the designer, albeit at some cost. If there is a concern that administrative costs may be too high for individual accounts, they could be administered by the Social Security Administration, which could offer a limited array of investment options to all at a very low cost, rather like a giant mutual fund. If there is a concern that the risks associated with the accounts are too high for an individual to bear, the government could guarantee a minimum level of return; indeed, almost all proposals for individual retirement accounts contain some type of guarantee. If there is a worry that low-income individuals would not fare well enough after retirement with individual accounts, given that the present system redistributes benefits toward the low income, their contributions can be subsidized. (There is an important policy issue as to whether subsidization should occur at the time when low-income people are putting money in or after they retire. The former approach will subsidize individuals who only have low incomes temporarily, like students and medical interns. On the other hand, the latter approach will be costly if it involves immediately improving the safety net for current retirees.)

The fact that individual accounts can be designed in so many different ways means that an enormous number of decisions about their structure are required. For example, should withdrawals after retirement be limited to a steady stream of income over time, like an annuity, or can larger lump sums be withdrawn? Should the level of withdrawals allowed differ by sex, given the different life expectancies of men and women? How should accounts be divided in the case of divorce? Practical questions of this type go on and on.

The economic and social effects of the final system will depend crucially on how such questions are answered.

Perhaps the fundamental economic concern about mandated individual savings accounts for retirement is how much they will actually increase savings. People can satisfy government mandates by diverting savings into the mandated accounts that would have otherwise gone into IRAs, 401ks, or other saving vehicles. Alternatively, they can both save more in the mandated retirement accounts and also borrow more, taking out larger mortgages or maintaining higher credit card balances so that their net savings does not change. However, it is also possible that if workers were required to set money aside, they would find at retirement that they had accumulated more than they would have expected, and more than they would have saved otherwise. Moreover, if a shift to individual accounts is accompanied by a reduction in the growth of Social Security benefits, this would create an additional incentive to save.

The major appeal of switching from a pay-as-you-go system to a system of funding and investment in equities is that the rates of return to contributions will probably be higher on average and less susceptible to demographic risks. The major appeal of funding the system privately is to reduce the prospects of the funds being used for political purposes. Many also favor individual accounts because of a desire to equalize the distribution of wealth. Relatively few people in the country today have even moderate financial wealth. There is, therefore, some philosophical appeal to making every person a capitalist through a system of personal retirement accounts.

A system of mandatory personal retirement accounts is sometimes referred to as "privatizing" Social Security, a term that is an ideological red flag to many conservatives and liberals—albeit for opposing reasons! Whatever one's views about privatization in other contexts, however, it is not appropriate to tote that baggage into this policy dispute. After all, a system of accounts where the size of the contributions is mandated by government, the investment choices are limited by government, and the withdrawal options are defined by government is hardly a "privatization" in any commonsensical definition of that word. (The alert reader will have noted that nowhere in the preceding paragraphs are mandatory personal retirement accounts described as "private" or "privatized.") Whether this lack of privatization is cause for jeremiads or jubilation, of course, is in the eye of the beholder.

A Fourth Social Security Proposal: President Clinton's Plan for Adding Debt to the Trust Fund

In early 1999, when President Clinton announced his proposed budget for fiscal year 2000, he offered a Social Security proposal that neither cuts benefits nor raises the present level of taxes. Instead, he proposed creating debt, by a stroke of the pen, that would be owed by the non–Social Security part of the government to the Social Security trust fund. The president's proposal would create an amount of debt equal to about 60 percent of projected unified budget surpluses, which is a way of selling the proposal politically to make it seem as though the budget surplus itself is somehow being deposited in the trust fund. But this is an illusion. A substantial portion of the budget surpluses are indeed due to Social Security—but those monies were already headed for the trust fund. The same debt that Clinton's plan adds to the Social Security trust fund could have been created for the trust fund even if there were no unified budget surpluses. Clinton's debt proposal essentially converts the implicit promise to pay future benefits, which already exists, into an explicit promise to pay future benefits, backed by federal debt, while doing nothing to address the issue of how to make the promised benefits affordable in terms of suggesting benefit reductions or tax increases.

President Clinton's plan jumbles together two separate goals: attempting to make sure the budget surpluses projected for the medium term are saved rather than spent on government programs or returned as a tax cut and building up the Social Security trust fund. Attempts to assure that the budget surplus is preserved to reduce the government debt and to add to national savings are a worthwhile idea. It will reduce the future interest bill on the national debt and so make it easier to afford the retirement of the baby boomers. A higher level of savings will also enhance economic growth, although, as noted earlier, higher economic growth does relatively little to fix the gap between projected Social Security revenues and benefits.

But there is no need to deposit the surpluses into the Social Security (or Medicare) trust funds to save the surplus. In fact, the act of depositing debt in the Social Security and Medicare trust funds is economically meaningless. As these programs grow relative to GDP, having additional debt in their trust funds in no way reduces the need to raise future taxes or cut benefits.

The act of adding debt to the Social Security trust fund is, however, more meaningful politically and philosophically. It amounts to a statement that Social Security and Medicare will no longer be largely financed by the earmarked payroll tax. If the Clinton proposal were to take effect, when the time comes for the Treasury debt deposited in the trust funds to be paid back, so as to finance future benefits, policy makers can redeem the debt by raising any federal tax (or by taking out more debt at that time). As a result, there would no longer be any presumption that Social Security or Medicare benefit payments should be related to payroll tax receipts over the long run. This transformation of the system would make Social Security much more like an ordinary tax-and-spend government benefit program.

Medicare, Medicaid, and Health Care for the Elderly

Government support for the health care expenses of the elderly through Medicare and Medicaid is less in the public eye than the debate over Social Security. But as America goes gray, these programs face potentially even more difficult problems.

Some key facts about the Medicare program are presented in Table 3. Medicare is divided into two main parts. Part A provides hospitalization services; everyone over age sixty-five is automatically eligible; and it accounts for about 70 percent of total Medicare spending. Part B provides physician services, and the elderly must pay a monthly premium to join. However, that premium covers only about one-third of the costs of Part B—which in turn is only about 30 percent of overall Medicare spending. Both Part A and B also require the payment of deductibles when receiving services.

The primary funding for the program is the 2.9 percent payroll tax (half paid by employees, half by employers), which is part of the deduction for FICA on every pay stub. Unlike Social Security, the Medicare payroll tax is not capped at a certain amount of income; it is collected on all earned income.

TABLE 3. About Medicare

Medicare has two parts:

Part A: Hospital Insurance	Provides coverage of inpatient hospital services, skilled nursing facilities, home health services.
Part B: Medical Insurance	Helps pay for the cost of physician services, outpatient hospital services, medical equipment and supplies, and other health services and supplies.

Medicare Outlays
[in millions of dollars]

Fiscal Year	Total	Part A	Part B	Medicare Premium Offsets	Net Medicare Outlays
1970	$7,149	$4,953	$2,196	($936)	$6,213
1980	35,034	24,288	10,746	(2,945)	32,089
1990	109,709	66,687	43,022	(11,607)	98,102
1998*	220,700	141,100	79,600	(21,200)	199,500

*CBO Projections (excludes discretionary spending)

Number of Eligible Enrollees and Beneficiaries, and Average Medicare Benefit
[beneficiaries in thousands]

Part A	1998 (est.)
Persons enrolled (monthly average)	38,561
Beneficiaries receiving reimbursed services	8,430
Average annual benefit per person enrolled*	$3,817

Part B	
Persons enrolled (monthly average)	36,906
Beneficiaries receiving reimbursed services	31,685
Average annual benefit per person enrolled*	$2,234

Sources: 1999. Health Care Financing Administration (HCFA), http://www.hcfa.gov/; and 1998 Green Book, Committee on Ways and Means, U.S. House of Representatives, Tables 2-1, 2-2.

Thus Medicare is a pay-as-you-go program in which current workers pay for the medical care of current retirees. It is exposed to exactly the same demographic issues as Social Security, that is, the number of recipients will grow rapidly after 2010. It faces the added problem that the cost of serving each recipient will also grow rapidly because health costs are likely to rise more rapidly than the overall price level. While the rise in health care costs was somewhat muted in the mid-1990s, with the rise of managed care, the primary factor driving such costs upward over time is the development of wonderful, life-preserving, and costly new technological innovations. With the ongoing revolutions in biology and genetics, the flow of such innovations does not seem likely to diminish. Thus a reasonable prognosis would be that while health care costs may not rise as rapidly as they did back in the 1970s and 1980s, it is still quite probable that they will rise more quickly than the general rate of inflation for years to come.

As a result of demographic and cost pressures, Medicare spending is projected by the Congressional Budget Office to rise from about 2 percent of GDP today to 6 percent of GDP by 2030—tripling its share of the overall economy. Since the revenue collected by Medicare payroll taxes is projected to rise only very modestly, an enormous gap will open up between Medicare revenues and spending. (In contrast, Social Security spending will rise more slowly relative to the size of the economy from about 4 percent of GDP at present to 6 percent of GDP by 2030.) Nevertheless, much of the discussion surrounding Medicare policy seems to be about guaranteeing new benefits as a trade-off for whatever other reforms may occur. It's certainly true that Medicare coverage is far from exhaustive. For example, it typically does not include prescription drugs, dental care, or long-term care. About a third of the elderly purchase other insurance to fill the gaps; the typical "Medigap" policy in a community rated plan cost about $1,300 in 1997. Others rely on employer health insurance coverage that extends into retirement, or on veteran's benefits, to cover the slack. But despite the evident gaps in Medicare, a system with promises growing far faster than its earmarked sources of revenue is not in much of a position to offer new benefits until the existing problems are resolved.

Medicaid is often discussed as a program for the poor (which is the context in which it arose in chapter 4). But the elderly can be poor, too. When they are, then Medicaid will pay their Medicare premiums and deductibles. Moreover, Medicaid covers some services not covered by Medicare, like nursing home care and pre-scription drugs. About one-third of Medicaid spending goes to the elderly, and that share is rising.

Figuring out how to address the health care costs of the elderly is a difficult task. Some of the proposals that could have a substantial impact on the Social Security picture, like raising the retirement age, won't do much for Medicare, because the bulk of the medical expenses for the elderly aren't incurred in the two or three years immediately after retirement but rather happen in the two or three years preceding death. To be sure, raising the eligibility age for Medicare might be a way to discourage early retirement, since some people would remain in their jobs to keep the health insurance benefits provided by employers. But this just means that the costs of health insurance are shifted to the private sector, which in turn might discourage firms from seeking to retain older workers.

Of course, a straightforward increase in payroll taxes on workers could do the trick. But a dramatic rise in Medicare payroll taxes on workers to balance the system would be a tough pill to swallow. The elderly could be required to pay more for their health care. But since they pay only about 10 percent of the total cost of Medicare now, even raising what the elderly pay by half would only cover 15 percent of the current costs of Medicare—not nearly enough to fill the looming fiscal gap. Moreover, even with Medicare in place, medical costs rose so quickly from the 1970s through the 1990s that out-of-pocket medical expenses by the elderly have risen from about 4 percent of average income in the mid-1970s to 8 percent of average income today.

If Medicare taxes are not raised very substantially, then at least part of the solution will need to be found in reducing costs, either by increasing efficiency or by reducing the quantity and/or quality of medical care received by the elderly. This is explosive political territory.

From non-economists, proposals are often heard for the government to impose lower prices on hospitals, doctors, and drug companies. This solution would seek to provide the elderly with just as much care as they receive now, but at a lower cost. But economists have learned to be wary of proposals for price controls. They can easily lead to poor quality of service, or to a high proportion of doctors and hospitals being unwilling to treat the elderly altogether. Holding down the price of today's drugs may sound attractive, but if in doing so the investment funds and the incentive for developing the drugs of tomorrow are eliminated, it's no longer such a good deal. Certainly, the government should negotiate hard with providers for the best possible price. But outside of truly radical solutions—like nationalizing the entire health care industry and criminalizing the private provision of medicine—such negotiations are unlikely to slash medical costs deeply and permanently.

Thus interest has turned to proposals that would give either patients or providers an incentive to hold down costs. One much discussed proposal, both for Medicare and for broader reform of health insurance markets, is Medical Savings Accounts (MSA). People would put a certain amount of money in an account each year, perhaps $2,000 or so. As an incentive for doing so, either the MSA contribution could come out of pre-tax income or interest on the money could be allowed to accumulate tax free. People would then purchase a catastrophic health insurance policy for any costs above that amount. At some point, if the money in the MSA was not used for medical care, then households would be able to use it for other purposes. As a result, individuals would have an incentive to hold down their usage of health care.

Proposals for Medical Savings Accounts are open to question on many grounds. How much would the use of medical care actually decline under such a system, given that the incentive is only to avoid smaller expenses, not larger ones? Are there some kinds of care, like regular preventive screening for certain maladies, where society would prefer that the elderly do not have an incentive for reducing health costs? If MSAs coexisted with Medicare, then it seems likely that healthy people would choose the MSA, so that they could eventually get some money back, while sick people would choose Medicare; but if the healthy are getting money back that would otherwise have stayed in the health care system, then the public cost of paying for the sick remaining in Medicare would rise. Politically, most people seem to favor additional medical insurance, not more exposure to the first several thousand dollars of costs.

An alternative way to encourage more efficiency in the delivery of health care, which was discussed in 1999 by a National Bipartisan Commission on the Future of Medicare, is to provide a fixed amount of assistance for the elderly to buy health insurance. The assumption is that the private sector would compete to offer attractive benefit packages at low cost. There is much disagreement about the likely effectiveness of such an approach, and the national commission found itself too divided to endorse such a plan. The main advantage of the commission approach is that government gains total control of costs—at least in theory. It can set the level of premium assistance at any level it desires, leaving beneficiaries the responsibility of bearing any extra costs. However, as a matter of practical politics, it is highly unlikely that government could sit back and require the elderly to bear a rapidly growing portion of their medical bills.

As with individual accounts for Social Security, there are many design details that must be resolved before a program of having the government pay fixed premiums could be implemented. For example, mechanisms have to be developed for having the government pay more according to age and health status; otherwise, companies will have an incentive to serve only the elderly who are most healthy. Mechanisms also have to be developed for addressing the vast differences in medical costs around the country, which vary a great deal according to local patterns of health care delivery. Spending per Medicare recipient in Miami is double that in Minnesota, with no apparent corresponding difference in the levels of illness or health among the recipients.

In the last few years, Medicare enrollees have received the option of joining a managed care company. The advantage of such a system for the government is that it pays a flat amount per individual, with actuarial adjustments for factors like age. Managed care firms participating in Medicare face certain rules about the basic level of services that must be provided. They are forbidden from making cash-back offers to enrollees, but encouraged to compete by expanding services. If managed care companies take any Medicare recipients at all, they must accept them without making any attempt to screen out the poorer health risks.

The hope of combining Medicare with managed care is that it will provide incentives to hold down costs while keeping the quality of service high. Since managed care firms receive only a flat amount per Medicare enrollee, they have an incentive to hold costs down. However, since managed care firms would be competing with each other to provide services, they should care about developing a reputation for good service. In 1997 60 percent of Medicare recipients lived in areas that provided a choice of at least two managed care plans, and one-third had a choice of five or more plans.

None of the proposals for dealing with Medicare look fully capable of dealing with the underlying issues. The long-term projections made by the trustees of the Medicare trust fund early in 1999 suggest that by the end of the seventy-five–year planning horizon, costs for the hospitalization (Part A) portion of Medicare will be literally double the income of the program. This projection arises without any expansion of Medicare to cover prescription drugs or other services.

The pending Medicare crisis is deep enough that the conventional agenda of reforms is unlikely to suffice. On the revenue side, Medicare taxes and cost sharing for the elderly can be increased to some extent, and on the cost side, experiments with greater use of managed care, Medical Savings Accounts, and tougher negotiations with health care providers may put some downward pressure on costs. But none of these common proposals, either individually or in combination, seems powerful enough to solve Medicare's long-term fiscal woes. Ultimately, the nation will be forced to come to grips with the reality that not every expensive medical innovation can always be available to every person at public cost.

Revisiting America's Intergenerational Compact

As the United States is forced by demography to reinvent its intergenerational compact, it is important to remember the successes of America's public policies regarding the elderly. In 1959, during the early years of Social Security and before Medicare was enacted, 35 percent of those over sixty-five fell below the poverty line. Even as recently as 1970, 25 percent of the elderly were poor. But today the poverty rate among the elderly has declined to 10 percent—less than the average poverty rate for the population as a whole. This is a remarkable social accomplishment. No one wants to return to the days when "elderly" was all too often synonymous with "poor." The United States is a wealthy society, and it can and should have social arrangements to assure that the elderly at least have a decent standard of living—and, indeed, that many will achieve a standard of living that is better than merely decent.

But continuing blithely along the present path is not an option, either. In effect, society is telling workers in their twenties and thirties and forties to pay for Social Security and Medicare today, even though the programs have a highly uncertain future and will not be able to continue as presently structured. The demographic crunch of an aging baby boom is coming, and it can not be sidestepped or ignored.

The compact between generations is not a one-way street in which working-age adults, now and in the future, will pay any amount that the political system has promised to the elderly. Assisting the elderly is not the only important goal of public policy, but rather must be balanced with support for young children, education, health care for others in the population, income assistance for the poor, national defense, law and order, and a number of other legitimate priorities—including private consumption. On current trends, Social Security and Medicare alone will grow from about 7 percent of the economy at present to 13 percent of the economy in 2030, as shown in Figure 9. The elderly are already absorbing more than half the noninterest, nondefense federal budget. That share is likely to continue to grow even with substantial reforms in Social Security and Medicare. If the elderly take such a substantial share of total government spending—and remember, these figures do not count private and family consumption directed toward the elderly—there will inevitably be less for all other purposes.

In the United States at the start of the twenty-first century, the assumption sometimes seems to be that a typical person will spend about twenty years growing to adulthood, perhaps forty years in the labor force, and then twenty years as a retiree—in other words, that people will earn income for about half of their lifetimes and be supported by a combination of family and government programs during the rest. If some people take time out of the workforce to raise children, or if they enter the workforce at more like age twenty-five and seek to retire at age fifty-five, then people would

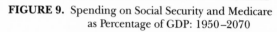

FIGURE 9. Spending on Social Security and Medicare as Percentage of GDP: 1950–2070

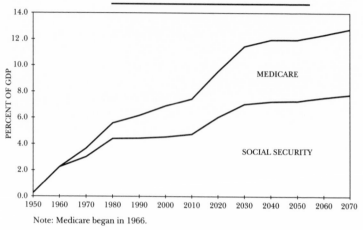

Note: Medicare began in 1966.

be earning income for much less than half of the average lifetime. It is not clear that this life pattern is fiscally sustainable, nor even desirable, nor that it is an implicit promise that the government should be attempting to fulfill for everyone.

The new intergenerational compact in the first few decades of the twenty-first century will require fixing Social Security and Medicare—but it will also require much more than that. It will probably also involve helping people save more as individuals. It will involve encouraging the elderly to stay on the job longer, through private sector efforts, government incentives, and shifts in social expectations. It will involve groping toward a new set of social, market, and political institutions to deal with a set of demographic patterns unlike those seen by any previous generation of Americans.

Uniting America
Leadership Advisory Group
(in formation)

Co-Chairs

David R. Gergen	*The NewsHour with Jim Lehrer*
Karen Elliott House	Vice President, International Group, Dow Jones & Company, Inc.
Donald F. McHenry	Georgetown University; Former U.S. Ambassador to the UN
Paul H. O'Neill	Chairman, ALCOA, Inc.

Members

Jonathan Alter	*Newsweek*
David E. Hayes-Bautista	School of Medicine, UCLA
Susan V. Berresford	President, The Ford Foundation
Derek Bok	Former President, Harvard University
David L. Boren	President, University of Oklahoma
Michael J. Boskin	Hoover Institution, Stanford University
Bill Bradley	former United States Senator
Joan Brown Campbell	General Secretary, National Council of Churches of Christ USA

Henry G. Cisneros	President and COO, Univision Communications, Inc.
Lee Cullum	Columnist, *Dallas Morning News*
Mario Cuomo	Former Governor of New York
Thomas R. Donahue	AFL-CIO
Peggy Dulany	President, The Synergos Institute
Don Eberly	President, The Civil Society Project, Commonwealth Foundation
Jeffrey A. Eisenach	President, Progress and Freedom Foundation
Marian Wright Edelman	The Children's Defense Fund
Dianne Feinstein	U.S. Senator
Jim Florio	Former Governor of New Jersey
David P. Gardner	President, The William and Flora Hewlett Foundation
John W. Gardner	Graduate School of Business, Stanford University
William George	Chairman & CEO, Medtronic
Peter C. Goldmark, Jr.	CEO, International Herald Tribune
Michael Goodwin	President, Office and Professional Employees International Union
William H. Gray III	President and CEO, United Negro College Fund, Inc.
Bryan J. Hehir, S.J.	Professor, Center for International Affairs, Harvard University
Antonia Hernandez	President and General Counsel, MALDEF
Irvine O. Hockaday, Jr.	President and CEO, Hallmark Cards, Inc.
Charlayne Hunter-Gault	*The NewsHour with Jim Lehrer*
Frank Keating	Governor of Oklahoma
Robert D. Kennedy	Retired Chairman, Union Carbide Corporation
James T. Laney	President Emeritus, Emory University
Sara Lawrence Lightfoot	Professor of Education, Harvard University

Bruce Llewellyn	Chairman and CEO, Philadelphia Coca-Cola Bottling Co.
Richard G. Lugar	United States Senator
David Mathews	President and CEO, Charles F. Kettering Foundation
Elizabeth McCormack	Trustee, John D. and Catherine T. MacArthur Foundation
William J. McDonough	President, Federal Reserve Bank of New York
Dana G. Mead	Chairman and CEO, Tenneco Inc.
Yolanda T. Moses	President, The City College of New York
Diana Natalicio	President, University of Texas at El Paso
Harry Pachon	Tomas Rivera Policy Institute
Robert D. Putnam	Professor of Political Science, Harvard University
Steven Rattner	Managing Director, Lazard Frères & Co.
Ralph Reed	Former Executive Director, Christian Coalition
Robert B. Reich	Brandeis University; former Secretary of Labor
William D. Ruckelshaus	Chairman and CEO, Browning Ferris Industries
George Rupp	President, Columbia University
Henry B. Schacht	Chairman and CEO, Lucent Technologies Inc.
Arthur Schlesinger, Jr.	Department of History, City University of New York
Adele Simmons	President, John D. & Catherine T. MacArthur Foundation
Alan K. Simpson	Former United States Senator
Edward Skloot	Executive Director, Surdna Foundation, Inc.
Theodore Sorensen	Paul, Weiss, Rifkind, Wharton & Garrison
Edson W. Spencer	Spencer Associates

Vin Weber	Former Congressman
Frank A. Weil	Chairman, Abacus & Associates, Inc.
John C. Whitehead	Chairman, AEA Investors Inc
William Julius Wilson	John F. Kennedy School of Government, Harvard University
Michael Woo	Director of Los Angeles Programs, LISC
Daniel Yankelovich	President, Public Agenda Foundation

Final Report
of the
Ninety-Fifth
American Assembly

The policy views expressed in the following Assembly report do not necessarily reflect the views of the authors of the preceding monograph nor the views of the trustees, officers, and employees of the Brookings Institution, the Urban Institute, or of The American Assembly.

At the close of their discussions, the participants in the Ninety-fifth American Assembly, on "The American Economy: Opportunity and Growth," at the Emory Conference Center, Atlanta, Georgia, June 10–13, 1999, reviewed as a group the following statement. This statement represents general agreement; however, no one was asked to sign it. Furthermore, it should be understood that not everyone agreed with all of it.

Preamble

The extraordinary strength of the U.S. economy provides an opportunity to focus on a better future for all Americans. This American Assembly on the economy seized the moment to address three long-term challenges that will greatly affect the degree of economic well-being in twenty-first century America.

The first challenge is to lay a strong foundation so that the economy continues to grow at a healthy pace with sustained full employment in the decades to come. At present, the winds of economic change have brought considerable economic good news. The economic expansion of the 1990s has been unusually long and robust. The unemployment rate has dropped to a thirty-year low without any acceleration of inflation. Productivity growth has accelerated in the late 1990s, and the stock market has boomed. A larger economy not only provides a higher standard of living and a greater range of opportunities, but also provides government with the resources to meet its commitments. For the economy of the future, growth must be built on a commitment to lifelong education, on greater investment in physical capital and scientific research, and on an open market environment in which innovation and entrepreneurship can flourish.

A second challenge is to assure that prosperity and the opportunities it brings are more broadly shared. America is an ocean of prosperity with too many islands of concentrated poverty. All children—in whichever neighborhood they live or whichever school they attend, whether urban, suburban, or rural settings—deserve the chance to acquire the education and skills required to participate in the mainstream of an increasingly technologically sophisticated economy. America must strive in many ways, in both the public and private sector, to bring the poor into the economic mainstream. This challenge reaches beyond the poor. All workers in the modern U.S. economy will find themselves facing powerful demands for building skills and for greater flexibility, and they require public and private institutions to help navigate in an economy that offers growth and opportunity, but demands readjustment, relocation, and lifelong learning.

The third challenge is the aging of the population and the impending retirement of the "baby boom" generation in the opening decades of the twenty-first century. Programs like Social Security and Medicare, which have been enormously successful in assisting the elderly, will come under increasing pressure as the elderly portion of the population increases and the size of the labor force stagnates. These issues are potentially divisive and explosive, and addressing them as a society will require recognizing the essential interdependence of successive generations. The structures of these programs, developed in the past, require rethinking. To be secure, the elderly must live in a society where economic growth is strong and their children and grandchildren are well-skilled and productive.

This American Assembly debated these three issues at length. We believe that our economy's future must be viewed in terms of the connections among all Americans—young and old; rich, poor, and middle class; rural, urban, and suburban; and long-time residents and recent immigrants—to provide a basis for reexamining America's social compact at the start of the twenty-first century. Following our deliberations, with the purpose of helping to unite America, this Assembly offers the following recommendations.

Nurturing High Employment and Growth

We believe that high employment, low inflation, and sustained economic growth are imperative not only because they bring prosperity and higher living standards to our nation as a whole, but also because they represent the foundation on which our other recommendations rest. A strong economy not only provides higher output and incomes, but also creates employment opportunities that in turn build attachments to the labor force, job experience, and a lasting base of skills. In particular, sustained expansion of employment brings into the mainstream of American economic life some of the long-term unemployed or welfare-dependent who would otherwise have remained on the fringe. Sustained growth also provides the resources required to finance other economic and social objectives, including enhanced educational and development opportunities for our children and dignified retirement for our senior citizens.

The economic expansion of the 1990s is the longest in peacetime during the twentieth century. Given the lowest unemployment rates seen since the 1960s, the economy has experienced much less wage and price inflation than many economists predicted. The Federal Reserve Board deserves considerable credit for pursuing a monetary policy that has allowed and encouraged the economy to continue growing, rather than succumbing to a fear that high employment must inevitably bring inflation—a fear that events have shown would have been misplaced. We urge the Federal Reserve to continue its pragmatic approach to monetary policy.

The nation's extraordinary recent economic performance has raised the question of whether the U.S. economy has entered a "new paradigm" that promises unprecedented increases in productivity and growth uninterrupted by recessions. We note that many American business leaders do, indeed, find themselves in a new economy. Globalization and other developments have intensified competition and produced relentless demands for higher productivity as a condition for business success—and even for survival. Reorganization of business structures and corporate downsizing have led to significant changes in the demand for workers, producing simultaneously both significant displacements and new opportunities.

We recognize that productivity gains during the last several years have been above the low rates commonly seen in the past three decades. Nevertheless, we are not persuaded that the new information and communications technology, combined with globalization and other forces, has transformed the economy into one that is recession-proof or inflation-proof, or in which nearly unprecedented productivity gains will characterize the future. Transformation is not a new experience for the U.S. economy; for example, this century has already experienced the economic revolutions of electrification, transportation, and telecommunications. Yet, in retrospect, it appears that certain lessons of economic policy continued to hold through those times. Many of these lessons offer guidance for the economic revolutions of today.

First and foremost among these lessons is that sustained, and especially more rapid, economic growth will require continued and enhanced investments in plant and equipment, in scientific research and applied technology, in the public infrastructure that provides a foundation for private activity, and, most especially, in education and training. A balanced mix of private and public investments will be needed to cultivate the seeds of future growth.

The recent advent of federal budget surpluses provides an extraordinary opportunity to mobilize national saving to finance these investments. Current mainstream projections, which do not assume unusual or accelerating economic growth, anticipate federal budget surpluses accumulating to $2.6 trillion over the next decade. We strongly believe that America must resist the temptation to use the projected surpluses for major tax cuts. Rather, a significant proportion of the surpluses should be retained as public saving through retirement of federal debt, which will free capital for private sector investment. The remainder should be used to seek out productive public investments at federal, state, and local levels of government. In this regard, however, we stress the importance of identifying and selecting public investments with high rates of return, which will genuinely enhance our economic growth, rather than—as too often happens—those that primarily satisfy political constituencies. We believe that these prudent, and indeed rather conventional, macroeconomic policies can lay a foundation to promote high employment and sustained, non-inflationary growth. In turn, economic health will improve the opportunities for all our fellow citizens to realize their potential for productive and satisfying lives—the ultimate end to which our policies must be directed. It is to that agenda for opportunity and fulfillment that we now turn.

Reducing Poverty and Increasing Opportunity

To ensure a more broadly shared prosperity, we emphasize the need to reduce poverty and to extend the opportunities available in the new economy to those who are currently most deprived. The high levels of income inequality across the population as a whole were also an important concern, although there was little sentiment for additional significant explicit redistribution of incomes. Yet we recognized the danger that too much inequality can lead to social tensions and undermine the nation's sense of cohesion.

There was also wide agreement that our society must seek a balance between rights and responsibilities. Society has certain obligations to take care of the needy, and individuals have a responsibility for their own well-being. As a result of the welfare reform legislation in 1996, almost all able-bodied individuals are now expected or required to work. To enhance the incentive to work and increase the income of the working poor, assistance should be made available to low-income individuals in such forms as child care, help with finding jobs, and earnings supplements.

In discussing the issues of poverty and inequality, we used the metaphor of a footrace. In America today, not everyone begins at the same starting line, some face special hurdles along the way, and not everyone finishes at the same place. We were especially concerned with equalizing the starting line, primarily through better education. But we recognized that history matters and that certain segments in our society, African-Americans in particular, still face higher hurdles that make it more difficult for them to participate fully in America's economic prosperity. Of special concern were continuing residential segregation, concentrations of inner city poverty that disproportionately impact minorities, and disparate treatment in the criminal justice system. We urge the forthcoming American Assembly on race to explore these issues.

Education

A well-educated workforce is the key to sustained growth in a high-tech economy. Too many of America's schools—together with the communities around the schools—are not presently rising to meet this challenge. While universal public education, a cornerstone of our democracy, has been primarily a local responsibility, increased globalization and the mobility of the population raise issues about whether this will be adequate in the future. We believe some re-alignment of national and local responsibilities is needed.

Strong educational development is increasingly a lifelong process. It must start in the earliest years of life. An accumulation of evidence indicates that stimulation of brain functioning in the first year and exposure to a rich language and visual environment have important long-term effects on child development. Programs to foster such an environment for children younger than age three are being tested and, if proved effective, should be extended to as many children as possible, especially those from low-income families. Education should then continue through an enriched pre-school environment. Pre-school programs have expanded in recent years, but coverage is far from complete and should be expanded further. No child should for reason of income be denied a strong pre-school experience. Increased pressure on the mothers of pre-school children to go to work should be accompanied by greater access to educationally oriented child care, and subsidization of such care should be provided to all low-income families.

The skills and habits of continual learning must then be fostered in the kindergarten through twelfth grade. Laments about the inadequacies of K-12 education have been widespread for at least a decade. Concerns about the state of education in the inner city are especially great. America needs a high school diploma that carries with it an assurance of a quality product. To this end, we recommend a strengthening of standards and greater accountability for the attainment of those standards.

America needs to establish national standards for what children should know and be able to do at different grade levels. High variations in local educational standards are intolerable. The ongoing pressures for higher skill levels and for ability to change jobs over one's career compel the nation to set standards, which, when achieved, will provide all school graduates with a firm basis for participating in the economy of the future.

With standards must come accountability for attaining those standards. Achieving and sustaining higher standards throughout America's schools will require realignment of school governance, consequences for nonperformance, adequate school resources and the ability to redeploy them, and retraining of teachers. Schools should be assessed on the basis of improvements in student achievement over a reasonable period of time.

Equal opportunity to attain these new national standards will require that a child from a poor community benefit from as high a level of resources as a child in a richer community. Thus, more equal funding per child is a critical component of the push to bring all graduates to competitive standards.

Approaches that combine career-focused education with apprenticeships and internships can motivate students, encourage a natural mentoring process, make career requirements more transparent, engage employers in training, and upgrade job opportunities.

The current school day and year ought to be extended, to ensure both that fewer children are left alone during after-school hours and that more time is devoted to instruction and developmental activities including sports, arts, community involvement, and work experience.

The education of our children is suffering in part because those who manage schools are not making the changes needed to affect school outcomes, such as substandard test scores. These administrators must be given the authority to make these changes, and they must be held accountable for the performance of their schools.

A variety of systemic changes should be explored to determine whether they address these problems equitably across school districts. The changes include greater choice between public schools—including charter and magnet schools—and perhaps even experiments with vouchers. Everyone—teachers, administrators, public officials, parents, and students—must be challenged and empowered to make changes that will meet the higher standards.

Changes in the U.S. economy require the development of new opportunities for skill-building after high school and a strengthening and expansion of public and private institutions for a lifelong emphasis on learning. Indeed, the returns to post-secondary education have risen sharply in the last two decades, showing how the market increasingly values the acquisition of additional skills. This emphasis on the acquisition of additional skills is especially relevant to workers of low and moderate income. Women's employment has increased to record levels, but many women continue to be stuck in low-wage jobs that make supporting a family impossible. The pressures of technological change are affecting even long-standing blue collar jobs. Thus, the post-secondary skill-building opportunities should be accessible not only to traditional post-secondary students, but also to those currently employed and seeking to move up the career ladder.

Assistance for the Working Poor

Existing cash and noncash benefits have substantially reduced poverty and hardship. This Assembly focused on the importance of ensuring that any additional assistance rewards work. In particular, a person with a family who works full time should be able to earn enough to exceed the poverty line and have access to adequate health care. This goal can be accomplished with a set of programs, including:

- *A moderate rise in the minimum wage.* Some participants strongly expressed a concern that this policy may reduce work opportunities.

- *Additional funding for the Earned Income Tax Credit (EITC).* This program has proved itself to be the most effective antipoverty program for working parents, providing a tax credit geared to the level of income earned by a family, with the amount rising to $3,700 for a parent with two children earning $10,000 per year. At higher income levels, the credit is phased out. Additional support for this program should be directed to phasing out the tax credit more slowly, so as to reduce the disincentive to work, and to allowing recipients of EITC benefits to marry without facing a dramatic reduction in benefits because their family income has increased.
- *Subsidizing child care costs.* Paying for child care represents a substantial part of the family budget for low-income working parents and has served as a barrier to employment, especially for single parents. Further, a society that requires women to leave welfare for work must also assure them of safe, affordable child care.
- *Further expansions of Medicaid* or other approaches to expanding health insurance for low-income Americans. Medicaid has already been expanded in recent years to cover the children of the working poor. It should also be expanded to include adults and families who are only a step or two above the poverty level.

Urban and Regional Issues

Improving the economic and social environment in America's large cities is critical to meeting two important goals: reducing poverty and improving the quality of life for city and suburban residents together.

We believe that it is important to strengthen institutions and infrastructure in our cities. The most important institution is public education, but other vital factors include improved transportation, housing, public safety, and community based organizations in the private economy. Businesses are beginning in some cases to recognize the opportunity to expand markets in central cities and to employ central city residents to meet their labor needs, as recommended by an earlier American Assembly report entitled

"Community Capitalism," but more remains to be done. Encouraging new entrepreneurs to start up and grow in central city neighborhoods can enliven these neighborhoods, give them resiliency, and spread the fruits of growth more broadly among the American people. Improving residential mobility is another way to increase the access of urban residents to better housing, jobs, and educational opportunities. For inner city residents who want this mobility, a combination of barriers exists, which must be overcome; these include the lack of affordable housing in the suburbs and social barriers related to race and ethnicity.

The health of America's cities is an important aspect of the nation's overall quality of life. Cities that are economically vibrant and are attractive places in which to live reduce the problems associated with urban sprawl and environmental pollution. Cities also provide opportunities to develop critically needed additions to the housing supply in metropolitan regions throughout America.

Entrepreneurship and Wealth Generation

In the increasingly competitive global economy, fostering entrepreneurship in the United States provides a key vehicle for economic progress. Public policy can encourage entrepreneurs to build businesses through the design of taxes and regulations. Some groups, especially women, African-Americans, and Latinos, are under-represented in business ownership for reasons of history, prejudice, or lack of access to the necessary capital. Encouraging entrepreneurship among these groups should enhance economic growth while increasing opportunity for these groups. Useful policies include providing effective business training, "extension-like" support services for new businesses, and improved access to capital, or even subsidized capital, to enable businesses to develop. The Empowerment Zone program is currently offering some of this support on a small scale in targeted urban and rural areas. We need to monitor these demonstration projects, so that successful programs or partnerships can be emulated.

Additional forms of asset development, such as home ownership, home improvement, and savings, are also important to enable all citizens to share in America's wealth. Savings can be encouraged through matching programs for low-income families, while home ownership and improvement can be encouraged through low-interest loans. Low-income communities are also under-served by financial institutions. The access of entrepreneurs and community development organizations to private capital can be enhanced through such policies as the Community Reinvestment Act.

Re-Assessing the Intergenerational Contract

Continued increases in life expectancy and the retirement of the baby boom generation will significantly increase the number of retirees relative to the number of workers in the next century. Between 2010 and 2030, the population over the age of sixty-five will rise 70 percent while the labor force is expected to rise only 4 percent. Under current law, the costs of the Social Security and Medicare programs will rise faster than the growth of the U.S. economy and far outrun the earmarked payroll taxes and premiums that now finance benefits. Current law is probably not sustainable for Social Security and is almost certainly not sustainable for Medicare. The important policy question involves distributing the burden of the changes that must be made. Possible options include raising taxes on the working population, on the benefits going to the elderly, or on the capital income of those already retired. Conversely, spending on other government programs could be cut to make room for an ongoing expansion of Social Security and Medicare, or the rate of projected growth in the real value of Social Security and Medicare outlays can be reduced. Pre-funding of some future retirement benefits should also be considered.

In addressing Social Security, this Assembly supports several proposals. The elderly should be encouraged to work longer, in particular by eliminating the earnings test for those aged sixty-five to sixty-nine. That test reduces benefits by one dollar for every three dollars above an exempt amount that rises to $30,000 by 2002. Gradually raising the normal age of retirement at which the elderly become eligible for Social Security benefits, in step with the ongoing rise in life expectancy, would also encourage the elderly to work longer. Finally, there was a broad sense that the affluent elderly should reasonably be asked to bear a larger share of the burden of adjustment. This Assembly recognizes that this combination of steps would not stabilize the economic burden imposed by the system, but only slow the rise in the costs. However, no consensus emerged on further reforms.

The Medicare system faces a financial crisis sooner than Social Security, and the size of the crisis will be larger than that of Social Security. However, the American public seems to focus on Social Security far more than on Medicare, and this American Assembly reflects that pattern as well. We agree that the current health care system does not deliver services as efficiently as it might. Medicare remains largely a fee-for-service system, with limited cost sharing and deductibles for patients, which encourages the over-use of medical care. America's health care system, like the K-12 education system, requires an institutional restructuring that would enhance incentives for efficiency. An example of a proposal that received cautious, but far from unanimous support, would have the government provide financial support to the elderly for the purchase of health insurance from private companies. The hope and intention of such a plan is that companies would compete for business and that the competition would lower costs and increase the quality of service. However, such a plan presents difficult administrative issues. Profit-making insurance companies would surely react to such a plan by trying to sign up only the healthiest of the elderly, leaving many of those who need medical care most with a government health care voucher that no company would wish to accept. This problem can be addressed through regulations, like adjusting the size of the vouchers according to the different health risks posed by different individuals and for regional differences in health care costs, and by making it harder for providers to screen the elderly. However, designing such regulations is a difficult task in itself, and the proliferation of such regulations will reduce the freedom of the market that the plan was intended to inculcate.

This Assembly urges that the more affluent pay a higher portion of their medical costs when retired. In particular, the affluent should pay a higher share of the costs of Part B Medicare, the insurance program that provides physician services. However, such "affluence testing" has to be structured carefully and limited in scope, so that it does not overly discourage individuals from saving for their own retirement.

In general, this Assembly does not feel an urgent need to solve immediately all of the public policy issues that will be posed by the aging of America's population, but it recognizes the necessity to begin implementing reforms as soon as possible. The longer such reforms are postponed, the more severe the changes that will ultimately be necessary.

Conclusion

Our vision for economic success in the twenty-first century encompasses prosperity for all Americans, with increased opportunity particularly for those traditionally marginalized. While based on a concern for the entire population, our deliberations have placed special emphasis on creating a prosperity that ensures for our children the start in life they need, and for our elderly the dignified retirement they deserve.

We believe that implementing our recommendations for action will create a better future and provide a solid foundation for uniting America.

Participants
The Ninety-Fifth American Assembly

MARCUS ALEXIS
Board of Trustees Professor of
    Economics
Professor of Management &
    Strategy
Northwestern University
Evanston, IL

STUART BRAFMAN
Investor
Chicago, IL

ROBERT BRAWER
Former President and CEO,
    Maidenform, Inc.
Author
New York, NY

RODNEY BROOKS
Deputy Managing
    Editor/Money
USA Today
Arlington, VA

GEORGE BUSBEE
Former Governor
    of Georgia
King and Spalding
Atlanta, GA

WILLIAM CHACE
President
Emory University
Atlanta, GA

PHOEBE H. COTTINGHAM
Senior Program Officer
Smith Richardson Foundation
Westport, CT

BRADLEY CURREY, JR.
Chairman
Rock-Tenn Company
Norcross, GA

HUGH M. DURDEN
President
Wachovia Corporation
Atlanta, GA

ESTER R. FUCHS
Director and Professor of Polit-
ical Science & Public Policy
Columbia University Center
for Urban Research & Policy
New York, NY

JAMES K. GALBRAITH
Professor
The University of Texas
LBJ School of Public Affairs
Austin, TX

††JAMES O. GIBSON
President
DC Agenda
Washington, DC

MICHAEL GRITTON
Policy Director
MassINC
Boston, MA

*HEIDI HARTMANN
Director and President
Institute for Women's Policy
Research
Washington, DC

**ROBINSON G.
HOLLISTER
The Joseph Wharton Professor
of Economics
Swarthmore College
Swarthmore, PA

RACHEL JONES
CEO
Child Wire, Inc.
Washington, DC

THOMAS J. KANE
Associate Professor of Public
Policy
Kennedy School of
Government
Harvard University
Cambridge, MA

ROSABETH MOSS
KANTER
The Class of 1960 Professor of
Business Administration
Harvard Business School
Boston, MA

JAMES LANEY
Former Ambassador to South
Korea
President Emeritus
Emory University
Atlanta, GA

JOHN LEOPOLD
Associate Director
Working Partnerships USA
San Jose, CA

ROBERT LERMAN
Director, Human Resource
    Policy Center
The Urban Institute
Professor of Economics
American University
Washington, DC

ROGER E. LEVIEN
President
Strategy and Innovation
    Consulting
Westport, CT

STEPHEN LEVY
Director
Center for Continuing Study
    of the California Economy
Palo Alto, CA

MARSHALL LOEB
Former Managing Editor
Fortune and *Money Magazine*
Editor
Columbia Journalism Review
Columbia University
Graduate School of Journalism
New York, NY

GERALDINE P. MANNION
Chair, Democracy Program
    and Special Projects
Carnegie Corporation of
    New York
New York, NY

MARY McCAIN
Vice President, Policy & Public
    Leadership
American Society for Training
    and Development
Alexandria, VA

DONALD F. McHENRY
Distinguished Professor of
    Diplomacy
Georgetown University
Washington, DC

CYNTHIA A. METZLER
Partner
Pepper Hamilton LLP
Washington, DC

JOEL MOTLEY
Managing Director
Carmona Motley Hoffmann
    Inc.
Tarrytown, NY

**CAROL O'CLEIREACAIN
Senior Fellow (Non-Resident)
The Brookings Institution
New York, NY

††JUNE E. O'NEILL
Wollman Professor of
    Economics & Director,
    Center for The Study of
    Business and Government
Baruch College, CUNY
New York, NY

†PAUL H. O'NEILL
Chairman
ALCOA, Inc.
Pittsburgh, PA

*VAN DOORN OOMS
Senior Vice President &
    Director of Research
Committee for Economic
    Development
Washington, DC

††MICHAEL WEINSTEIN
Economics Columnist
The New York Times
New York, NY

MICHAEL WOO
Director of Los Angeles
    Programs
Local Initiatives Support
    Corporation (LISC)
Los Angeles, CA

About The American Assembly

The American Assembly was established by Dwight D. Eisenhower at Columbia University in 1950. It holds nonpartisan meetings and publishes authoritative books to illuminate issues of United States policy.

An affiliate of Columbia, The Assembly is a national educational institution incorporated in the state of New York.

The Assembly seeks to provide information, stimulate discussion, and evoke independent conclusions on matters of vital public interest.

American Assembly Sessions

At least two national programs are initiated each year. Authorities are retained to write background papers presenting essential data and defining the main issues of each subject.

A group of men and women representing a broad range of experience, competence, and American leadership meet for several days to discuss the Assembly topic and consider alternatives for national policy.

All Assemblies follow the same procedure. The background papers are sent to participants in advance of the Assembly. The Assembly meets in small groups for four lengthy periods. All groups use the same agenda. At the close of these informal sessions participants adopt in plenary session a final report of findings and recommendations.

Regional, state, and local Assemblies are held following the national session at Arden House. Assemblies have also been held in England, Switzerland, Malaysia, Canada, the Caribbean, South America, Central America, the Philippines, Japan, China, and Taiwan. Over one hundred sixty institutions have cosponsored one or more Assemblies.

Arden House

The home of The American Assembly and the scene of the national sessions is Arden House, which was given to Columbia University in 1950 by W. Averell Harriman. E. Roland Harriman joined his brother in contributing toward adaptation of the property for conference purposes. The buildings and surrounding land, known as the Harriman Campus of Columbia University, are fifty miles north of New York City.

Arden House is a distinguished conference center. It is self-supporting and operates throughout the year for use by organizations with educational objectives. The American Assembly is a tenant of this Columbia University facility only during Assembly sessions.

Index